SOLVING THE *MYSTERIES* OF THE DEAD SEA SCROLLS

SOLVING THE *MYSTERIES* OF THE DEAD SEA SCROLLS

New Light on the Bible

EDWARD M. COOK

ZondervanPublishingHouse
Academic and Professional Books
Grand Rapids, Michigan

A Division of HarperCollins*Publishers*

Solving the Mysteries of the Dead Sea Scrolls

Requests for information should be addressed to:
Zondervan Publishing House
Academic and Professional Books
Grand Rapids, Michigan 49530

All the translations contained herein are the author's own, except where otherwise noted.

Edited by Patricia H. Picardi
Cover designed by John M. Lucas
Cover photo by Photo Edit
Map by Louise Bauer

Printed in the United States of America

Library of Congress Cataloging-in-Publication Data

Cook, Edward M.
Solving the mysteries of the Dead Sea scrolls : new light on the Bible / Edward M. Cook.
p. cm.
Includes bibliographical references.
ISBN 0-310-38471-0
1. Dead Sea scrolls—Criticism, interpretation, etc. 2. Dead Sea scrolls—Relation to the New Testament. 3. Bible. N.T.—Criticism, interpretation, etc. 4. Christianity—Origin. 5. Qumran community. I. Title.
BM487.C58 1994 93-39075
296.1'55—dc20 CIP

94 95 96 97 98 99 / CH / 10 9 8 7 6 5 4 3 2

To the memory of

Paul King Jewett
and
William Sanford LaSor

teachers of righteousness

Contents

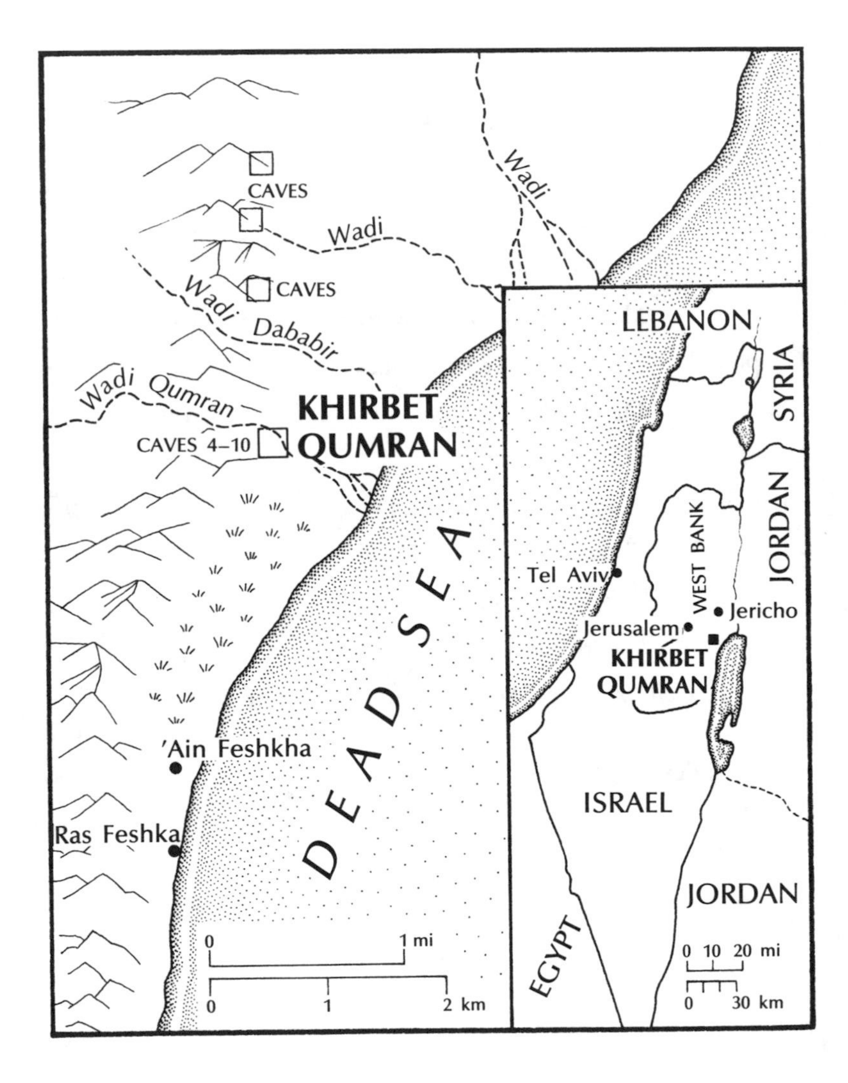
CAVES
Wadi
Wadi
CAVES
Wadi Dababir
Wadi Qumran
KHIRBET QUMRAN
CAVES 4–10
DEAD SEA
'Ain Feshkha
Ras Feshka
0 1 mi
0 1 2 km
LEBANON
SYRIA
JORDAN
WEST BANK
Tel Aviv
Jericho
Jerusalem
KHIRBET QUMRAN
ISRAEL
JORDAN
EGYPT
0 10 20 mi
0 30 km

Preface

The Dead Sea Scrolls have been rediscovered. Many are already familiar with some of the events that led to a new era of study of those scrolls that had remained unpublished and in private hands. New access to the photographs and transcriptions of the unreleased scrolls, along with public controversies that have attended that access, has heightened interest to a level not seen since the first discoveries. It is in this sense that I speak of a "rediscovery."

But it is not just the lay public whose interest has been piqued. Many scholars who believed they would never see the unpublished scrolls have turned with renewed vigor to a subject that, five years ago, seemed tired and played out.

That is what happened to me. As a specialist in Aramaic and Hebrew, I have had the chance to pore over photos of ancient texts that I never knew existed from the period when those languages were the medium of a thriving literary culture and the church was being conceived. My heart literally beat faster as I began to work on these tattered fragments. This book has its origin in my own racing pulse.

It also starts from (and ends in) a recognition of the bewildering complexity of the historical and religious issues the Dead Sea Scrolls raise. It is the scrolls' effect on the understanding of the New Testament that has awakened the most interest, and, in my opinion, has most deformed the public conversation about these fascinating documents. I have encountered many people who hope the scrolls will provide new revelations. Some want the scrolls to knock the props out from under Christianity. Others hope they will provide crucial evidence supporting the New Testament, enabling the faithful to slay the doubts of the unbelievers once and for all.

In such a fervid climate of opinion, I want to join the vast majority of specialists in saying that this is not what the scrolls are about. Every new manuscript discovery has something of the character of a "word from beyond": beyond our own time, beyond the limitations of the historical evidence we had grown to accept as immutable. It is natural to expect disclosures that will settle some questions once and for all. In some areas, the scrolls have done just that; but, by and large, the scrolls have left us with many more questions than answers. This book tries to make clear exactly what the Dead Sea Scrolls can and cannot tell us, while emphasizing those areas of the debate that I judge to be of most interest to my fellow Christians.

Finally, the story of the scrolls and their discovery is a narrative rich in excitement and mystery, with the best and worst of human nature on display. I have tried to update that story in brief compass as impartially as possible.

Although the scholarly discussion on the scrolls has sometimes been marred by rancor, the Qumran scholars I talked to have been, without exception, generous, cordial, and helpful. I must particularly thank here the following gentlemen for answering many questions and correcting many errors: Prof. Robert Eisenman, to whom I am indebted for a number of items from his personal files; Dr. Weston Fields; Fr. Joseph A. Fitzmyer, S. J.; Dr. David Gilner; Mr. Hans van der Meij of E. J. Brill, Leiden, Holland; Prof. Waverly Nunnally; Prof. James Robinson; Prof. Lawrence Schiffman; Mr. Hershel Shanks; Prof. John Strugnell; Prof. Emanuel Tov; Prof. Eugene Ulrich; Prof. Ben-Zion Wacholder; Prof. Michael O. Wise; and Prof. Bruce Zuckerman. I owe a special debt of thanks to Dr. Martin G. Abegg, Jr., for his unselfish help, his many insights, and his friendship.

None of those named are responsible for any errors of fact or interpretation that remain.

Special thanks also go to Dr. Jerome A. Lund, Dr. Steven Boyd, and Prof. Stephen A. Kaufman, my colleagues at the Comprehensive Aramaic Lexicon Project at Hebrew Union College, for their encouragement and interest in this book. I am indebted to the staff of the Klau Library at Hebrew Union College, in particular Mrs. Dana Frederickson and Mr. Richard Hedrick; their patience is as endless as the resources of the Klau itself.

My last and largest thanks go to my long-suffering family, in particular my wife Laura: *at `alit `al kullanah* (Prov. 31:29).

Chapter 1

The Discovery of the Dead Sea Scrolls, 1947–1960

The central scene of the most famous archaeological discovery of the twentieth century is this: A man puts a lighted torch into a dark space and peers into it. Another man standing behind him asks, "Can you see anything?"

"Yes," says the man with the torch. "Wonderful things."

The year is 1922. The man is, of course, archaeologist Howard Carter, who has just discovered the tomb of Tutankhamen. If his discovery is still more celebrated than the discovery of the Dead Sea Scrolls, it is partly because of the perfection of this scene, which has everything a great discovery should have: a torch, a dark hole, a fabulous treasure. On another level, it also symbolizes our romance with the darkness of our human past, into which we are always seeking to thrust a torch and find wonderful things.

Unfortunately—at least for our sense of romance—the greatest discoveries are often made quite by accident. So it was with the Dead Sea Scrolls. At the beginning of the story there was a cave, and in it were wonderful things, but there the resemblance ends. A young Bedouin shepherd, Muhammad edh-Dhib, stumbled upon the cave while looking for a lost sheep in the barren foothills of the Judean wilderness near the north shore of the Dead Sea. In the course of this (almost biblical) errand, he tossed a stone into an opening in the rock. Instead of the bleat of a trapped animal, he heard the sound of breaking pottery. Intrigued, he entered the cave and found elongated jars of clay. Inside these vessels were leather scrolls with writing on them.

That story is honored by long repetition, but there are other versions of it. In one rendition, the boy and a companion went into the cave to take shelter from a storm. In another, someone else threw the rock, and then the boy entered the cave. In still another, several Bedouin were up to no good—possibly smuggling goods from Transjordan to Bethlehem—when they found the cave. (In another variation, the flock itself was the contraband.) There is also some confusion about when the discovery actually took place. February 1947 is a date commonly given, but winter 1946 has also been suggested. Muhammad edh-Dhib, now more than seventy years old and known as Abu Dahoud, has recently revised the date to 1936![1] In any case, the Bedouin and other members of his Taamireh tribe returned to the site the next day and removed a number—possibly seven—of the scrolls. They did not consider these grimy objects to be "wonderful things," much less "the greatest manuscript discovery of modern times," as they came to be known.

> We kept them lying around the tent, and the children played with them. One of them broke into pieces and we threw the pieces on the garbage pile. Later we came back and found that the wind had blown all the pieces away.[2]

Yet they knew that Western scholars valued ancient objects. The scrolls might fetch a certain amount of money on the antiquities market. If not, they might serve as sandal straps. . . .

The Bedouin carried the scrolls around for a few months or possibly years, before doing anything with them. No one recognized the strange writing. Someone suggested that it was Syriac, a form of Aramaic, a language related to Hebrew and Arabic and written in a flowing script. Perhaps a merchant who also knew Syriac could tell them if their scrolls were worth anything.

So the Bedouin took their scrolls to a cobbler cum antiquities dealer in Bethlehem known as Kando (real name: Khalil Iskander Shahin). Kando in turn notified a friend in Jerusalem, George Isaiah, who was a member of the Syrian Orthodox Church, which still uses Syriac in its liturgy. Together they took some pieces torn from the scrolls to the Syrian Orthodox Archbishop of Jerusalem, Mar Athanasius Yeshue Samuel. It was April 1947.

Treasure of Qumran

Mar Samuel is a key figure in the early days of the discovery. Some have cast his motives and actions in the worst possible light—partly because they felt that he had not been completely candid with all parties involved.[3] One thing, however, is clear: If Mar Samuel had not acted as he did, Kando would likely have used the greatest manuscript discovery of modern times to repair shoes in his cobblery, and no one else would ever have seen them. Mar Samuel recognized that the scrolls were written in Hebrew, not Syriac. Though no authority on antiquities, and suspecting fraud, he thought they might be authentic ancient manuscripts. He asked the two men to bring all the scrolls they had; he would like to buy them. Kando and Isaiah went away, promising to return.

But when the antiquities dealers and their clients returned to Jerusalem in mid-July, they were at first turned away by the gatekeeper at St. Mark's Monastery, where Mar Samuel lived and worked. When he found out about the mistake and got back in touch with Kando, he was told that some of the Bedouin, miffed at their treatment, had taken a few scrolls elsewhere. The archbishop persuaded the others to bring the rest of the scrolls by the monastery, however; and, according to his version of the story, he gave his entire life savings to acquire them—about $250.

Having thus gambled what was, for him, a significant amount of money on the scrolls, the archbishop set out to establish their authenticity. He contacted academics, archaeologists, and bureaucrats, including one from the Department of Antiquities—anyone he thought might be an expert. Most were skeptical; none were encouraging. Why? Critic Edmund Wilson, in his celebrated book on the Dead Sea Scrolls, gives a cynical answer:

> [T]here is . . . at work here the natural instinct to simplify one's scholarly problems by establishing a closed field. One likes to feel that one has seen all the evidence. One has mastered it and worked out one's theories; and it is very upsetting—especially, if one suffers from

> imaginative limitations—to have to be obliged to deal with new material.[4]

Wilson himself apparently suffered from no imaginative limitations if he thought that any scholar interested in ancient history would not give his or her right arm for authentically ancient documents, previously unknown, regardless of how they might affect one's own theories. To publish or even to read such manuscripts is the Holy Grail of scholarship—a chance so coveted that it led to fierce scholarly strife in the later history of Dead Sea Scrolls research. Wilson was wrong. In 1947 there was hardly a scholar in the world, even Jerusalem, who could recognize Jewish manuscripts from pre-Christian times—because, before 1947, few such manuscripts were known. And besides, the idea of finding such a manuscript was just too good to be true, and therefore probably wasn't.

Meanwhile, the other Bedouin, the ones Kando and the archbishop were unable to mollify, took a batch of three scrolls to yet another antiquities dealer in Bethlehem. This man, Feidi Salahi, got in touch with his own expert, the professor of archaeology at the Hebrew University in Jerusalem, E. L. Sukenik.

At the time, Sukenik was possibly the only man in the country who specialized in Jewish paleography—the study of ancient writing. He had made a particular study of the inscriptions found on ossuaries, or bone-boxes. In the first century A.D. and earlier, the Jews would make room for additional interrals in their tombs or mausoleums by removing the remains of previous burials, and reverently storing the disjointed skeletons in decorated boxes. They would scratch the name of the deceased on the outside and store them away. Sukenik had studied many of the ancient ossuaries of Jerusalem and the Hebrew script of the epitaphs.

Jerusalem was under a curfew and divided into different security zones at the time Sukenik was contacted by an Armenian friend acting on Salahi's behalf. The British, who were in control of Palestine, had restricted Jewish immigration for fear of further aggravating Arab-Jewish tensions. Infuriated, the Jews of Palestine had begun a violent campaign of terror against the British. Hoping to put a lid on the growing disorder, the British began in March 1947 to string barbed wire around the Jewish communities in northwestern Jerusalem and to demand military passes to move from one zone to another.

When the Armenian called Sukenik to offer him certain unnamed "items of interest," the scholar was curious, but, without a military pass, unable to go out of his zone. The Armenian likewise was unable to pass in to see Sukenik, so they agreed to meet on November 24 at the sentry checkpoint and to converse over the barbed wire.

"The Letters Began to Become Familiar"

The Armenian explained that he had some fragments taken from manuscripts discovered by Bedouin near the Dead Sea. When Sukenik took a closer look at the leather scrap the man brought out of his bag, he forgot, for the moment, about the barbed wire.

> Strangely enough, as I gazed at the parchment, the letters began to become familiar, though I could make no immediate sense of the writing. They resembled letters which I had found on several occasions on small coffins and on ossuaries which I had discovered in and around Jerusalem, in some ancient tombs dating back to the period before the Roman destruction of the city [A.D. 70]. I had seen such letters scratched, carved and, in a few cases, painted on stone. But not until this week had I seen this particular kind of Hebrew lettering written with a pen on leather.
>
> My first thought was that this was possibly the work of some forger, who had conceived the idea of imitating the script on leather. But this thought stayed with me for barely a moment. As I continued to peer, my hunch became stronger and stronger that this was no forgery but the real thing.[5]

Mar Samuel suspected and hoped; Sukenik was beginning to be sure. Sukenik told the Armenian he was very interested in the scrolls, but first he wanted to see more than just the sample fragment. He managed to get a military pass and on November 27 went to the Armenian's house. There he examined several more fragments, and, now firmly convinced of their authenticity, agreed to go to Salahi's shop in Bethlehem to purchase all the materials.

It was a dangerous time for a Jew to travel deep into the Arab sector, where Bethlehem was located. Arab-Jewish tensions remained high. All of Palestine was in an agony of suspense, waiting for the United Nations to decide on the political fate of the Holy Land after the approaching end of British rule.

Sukenik asked his older son for advice. His son was doubly qualified to serve as his father's confidant; for he was himself not only a trained archaeologist but also Chief of Operations of the Haganah, the Jewish underground military organization. As a first-generation Israeli, he had given up his father's Hungarian surname and proudly assumed a Hebrew name: Yigael Yadin. Although nearly as excited about the scrolls as his father, Yadin joined his mother in pleading with Sukenik not, on any account, to venture into Arab territory.

Nevertheless, Sukenik slipped out on the 29th to meet the Armenian dealer, and the two of them took the bus to Bethlehem. There, at Salahi's shop, Sukenik saw two complete scrolls, as well as two of the jars which had contained them. He begged to be allowed to examine the scrolls at home.

Sukenik returned home with the scrolls just before a storm of emotion broke over Jerusalem. That night the United Nations voted to partition Palestine into two states—one Jewish, one Arab. Jews everywhere poured into the streets to celebrate, defying the curfew, while Arabs mourned. Both sides began to prepare for war. Sukenik tore himself away from his desk, where the scrolls were spread out for study, to go outside and celebrate with the rest of the Jews. He was celebrating not only the partition decision, but his new find as well. He felt it was divinely ordained that the scrolls should come to light at the very moment of the birth of Israel.

The next day Sukenik returned to his desk, and stayed there for months, poring over the scrolls. He got the purchase money to Salahi and made one more foray to the shop in December to purchase another scroll, making a total of three.

In the meantime, Archbishop Samuel had continued to seek either buyers for the scrolls or experts who could assess their value, but in vain. Finally, in January 1948, Samuel desperately turned to one of his well-to-do parishioners, one Anton Kiraz, for advice. Kiraz offered to contact an archaeologist of his acquaintance from the Hebrew University—Prof. E. L. Sukenik.[6]

Kiraz, on behalf of Samuel, contacted Sukenik by mail in late January 1948. The note took three days to travel less than two miles, but it got there. Since Partition Night, conditions had deteriorated in Jerusalem; terrorism, sniping, and bombings were daily occurrences, despite the continuing presence of the British troops. Food and fuel were scarce for the Jewish community of Jerusalem, cut off from their sources of supply by the predominantly Arab countryside. A correspondent for the *New York Times* said, "Jerusalem is becoming virtually isolated behind a curtain of fear. No one comes to Jerusalem or leaves his neighborhood except for an emergency."

So it was with some amazement that Arabs using the YMCA library on February 4 watched a tall Jew enter with some books under his arm, apparently having made the dangerous journey from the Jewish sector merely to return some books. In fact, it was Sukenik, who had set up a meeting with Kiraz at a private room at the YMCA; the books were a cover. Kiraz had brought the St. Mark's scrolls for Sukenik's perusal.

Sukenik, who had spent the last few months studying the material he bought from Feidi Salahi, could see right away that the St. Mark's scrolls were similar to his own collection. As with Salahi, he received permission to examine the scrolls at his leisure, and spent the next few days frantically trying both to study the new texts and raise money to buy them. He wanted cash, guessing that Kiraz and Samuel, even if dissatisfied with the amount of the offer, would not turn down cash on the table. He failed to raise the money, but returned to the YMCA days later with the scrolls and an offer. Kiraz took the scrolls, promising to consider the offer, made an appointment with Sukenik for the following week, and left. Sukenik never saw him again.

What happened? Samuel decided to refuse Sukenik's offer. The archbishop's reasons are not entirely coherent:

> [T]hough the interest of the [Hebrew] university was revitalizing, it still did not answer my questions: *What* were they? *Where* did they come from originally? *How* did they come to be in a cave in the Dead Sea wilderness? That a scholar was interested in purchasing them was good news indeed, but it was the secrets of the scrolls themselves that fascinated me. I advised Anton to inform me of any further word he would have from the university, but I was not completely satisfied that this should be their final disposition.[7]

But Kiraz and Sukenik both stated that another meeting was already scheduled, not that Kiraz would wait for further word. And clearly Mar Samuel could not expect his questions about the scrolls to be answered immediately, regardless of who his expert was. The underlying reason for refusing Sukenik's offer may have been that it was disappointingly low—$2,025 according to Kiraz, although considerably more than Samuel had paid. Another reason may have been that, at a time when Jewish-Arab violence was increasing, Mar Samuel didn't want to sell his treasure to the Jews.

"Not the Slightest Doubt in the World"

On the morning of February 18, 1948, a young American scholar was at the Palestine Archaeological Museum photographing scarlet anemones for a course on "Flora of the Bible." He was snapping pictures against a background of far-off gunfire, which caused him only to crouch down lower behind the garden wall. Within twenty-four hours the anemones would be forgotten, and the cameras would be used for far more important tasks.

The scholar was thirty-two-year-old John C. Trever, then acting director of the American Schools of Oriental Research (ASOR). Founded in 1900, ASOR is a daughter organization of three American institutions devoted to biblical and archaeological research: the American Oriental Society, the Society of Biblical Literature, and the American Institute of Archaeology. It organizes and coordinates various biblical and archaeological research projects from its two centers in Jerusalem and Baghdad. In 1948, the Jerusalem center was simply struggling to maintain a semblance of its normal work in the midst of the Arab-Jewish conflict—hence Trever's innocuous pastime at the museum. The director of ASOR, Dr. Millar Burrows of Yale, was away visiting the Baghdad center; Trever and another scholar, William Brownlee, were—almost literally—holding down the fort until Burrows' return.

That afternoon Trever received a phone call from St. Mark's. The monk on the other end said that St. Mark's had been cataloguing their library and had come across some Hebrew scrolls. The monk wondered if Dr. Trever could give an opinion on their age and value. Trever agreed, and they set an appointment at the ASOR building.

The next day Father Butrus Sowmy of St. Mark's, with his brother Ibrahim, a minor customs official for the British government in Palestine, arrived to meet Trever. They brought out five scrolls for his examination. One of them was in an advanced state of decomposition, and two others were too brittle to unroll easily. But one large scroll unrolled readily. Trever recognized the script as Hebrew, but of a kind unfamiliar to him. While the Sowmys waited nervously, Trever examined photographs of ancient manuscripts to compare the scripts. The closest match to the scroll in front of him was a picture of the Nash papyrus, a scrap of text containing the Ten Commandments and dated to the first or second century B.C.

B.C.! If Trever's eye had not misled him, the scroll he held was as old as the Nash papyrus, yet much larger, much more important, and much more valuable. Trever, unlike some of the previous consultants to St. Mark's, was more afraid of losing a historic opportunity than of being fooled by a hoax. He assured the men of his interest, and said he would contact them soon with a considered opinion on the age and value of the manuscripts. Before they left, Trever copied part of the large scroll for later study.

That night, he and Brownlee determined that the segment Trever had copied was from chapter 65 of the book of Isaiah. The ancient scroll was a copy of Isaiah. Later Trever wrote:

> Sleep was almost impossible that night. Numerous questions flooded my mind. How long was the large scroll? How much of Isaiah was there? Could it be authentic? . . . But how could such a perfect manuscript be as old as the Nash papyrus? Out of sheer exhaustion I fell asleep, still arguing with myself.[8]

The next day Trever hurried to St. Mark's and asked the archbishop to let him take pictures of the scrolls. Mar Samuel consented, perhaps impressed by Trever's youthful enthusiasm, not to mention his hints at the great monetary value of the scrolls.

Over the next week or so Trever, a photography buff since his Boy Scout days, took pictures of each column of writing on each scroll, except for the badly decomposed fifth scroll, which could not be unrolled. Aided by Brownlee, Trever repaired cracks in the ancient leather with Scotch tape. The two scholars discovered in the course of this work—which was supervised by the wary St. Mark's monks—that two of the scrolls were actually part of one scroll; it had been broken since its discovery in the cave. (The scroll would later be known as the *Manual of Discipline*.) In studying the pictures the two scholars became more and more convinced of the great age of the scrolls. Trever dashed off a letter with two prints of the Isaiah scrolls to America's most prominent biblical archaeologist, W. F.

Albright of the Johns Hopkins University. If the great Albright were to concur with their theories, then half the battle of convincing the rest of the scholarly world would be over.

When Burrows returned to Jerusalem on February 28, Trever and Brownlee eagerly informed him of their discovery. Although reserved at first, he was quickly convinced of the scrolls' antiquity and caught the younger scholars' excitement. As director, Burrows quickly assumed command of the American "team" dealing with the scrolls.

Millar Burrows was not himself an archaeologist, but a specialist in the Old Testament. He had, however, a happy talent for communicating the results of modern research in language understandable to the public. Moreover, one of his goals for ASOR was to enhance the stature of American scholarship. He felt that American monetary support for research in the Middle East was being used too much to underwrite the work of foreign scholars and that American brainpower was, as a result, being neglected.[9] There was therefore probably an element of boosterism when Burrows began to think of two courses of action: to write a press release revealing to the world the American discovery of the oldest biblical manuscript, and to secure for ASOR the rights to publish the photographs. Such a publication would be a signal accomplishment for, if not a vindication of, American biblical scholarship.

The St. Mark's people would have to be convinced, however. Mar Samuel was still waiting for a definitive judgment on the age and value of his property. The ASOR team assured him they were convinced of the scrolls' antiquity but that much detailed and public discussion by qualified scholars would be necessary to establish the age, and therefore the price, of the documents. Apparently it began to dawn on the archbishop that his manuscripts could not simply be appraised in one sitting like diamonds under a jeweler's eyepiece. He agreed to let Burrows release an announcement to the press and to let ASOR have publication rights to his scrolls.

From this point—March 1948—events move rapidly. Trever received a letter from Albright saying:

> My heartiest congratulations on the greatest manuscript discovery of modern times! There is no doubt whatever in my mind that the script is more archaic than that of the Nash Papyrus . . . I should prefer a date around 100 B.C. . . .

> I repeat that in my opinion you have made the greatest manuscript discovery of modern times—certainly the greatest biblical manuscript find. . . . Burrows will now have a chance to forget the events in Palestine for a while. Let us hope that nothing happens to your precious finds! . . . You can imagine how my eyes bulged when I saw the script through my magnifying glass! What an absolutely incredible find! And there can happily not be the slightest doubt in the world about the genuineness of the manuscript.

Albright's expression "the greatest manuscript discovery of modern times" came to be repeated again and again, partly because it was Albright who said it, partly because it was true. But, glad as they were to have Albright's support, the ASOR team was worried about another topic mooted in Albright's letter: the possibility of something happening to the scrolls.

This was no idle worry. Jerusalem was becoming increasingly violent. On February 21, fifty-four Jews were killed by an Arab bomb on Ben Yehuda Street. On March 11, eleven were killed and eighty-six wounded by another bomb set at the Jewish Agency. On April 9, hundreds of Arabs, including women and children, were killed in the village of Deir Yassin by renegade Jewish forces. The country was rapidly unraveling toward full-scale hostilities as the end of British rule—May 15—approached. The prospect of the scrolls being seized or destroyed was very real.

Not only that, but Sukenik had learned to his dismay that the St. Mark's scrolls were in the hands of ASOR. He believed that those scrolls had been promised to him, or at least that he had the right of first refusal. Besides, were they not Jewish scrolls? Unlike Trever, Sukenik had not had to spend an entire night discovering that the large scroll was Isaiah. With his intimate knowledge of the Old Testament, he had recognized it instantly. It was only fitting for the scrolls to belong to the new nation of Israel.

The ASOR team was determined to hold on to the scrolls. What role anti-Jewish or anti-Zionist feeling played in this decision is not clear. Burrows was ardently opposed to the establishment of the Jewish state and deeply sympathetic to the Palestinian cause; a year later, he resigned his ASOR post in order not to compromise the organization's political neutrality. In his book *Palestine Is Our Business* (1949), Burrows comes close to anti-Semitism in certain expressions.[10]

Nevertheless, in his actions at this time and in later publications dealing with the scrolls, there is no evidence that he was acting from any motive other than concern for the scrolls' physical safety, and possibly a sense of professional competition with Sukenik (who was himself associated with ASOR in the twenties—perhaps one of the "foreigners" whose activities so rankled Burrows!).

Burrows and Trever had been urging the archbishop to take the scrolls out of the country. This idea suited Mar Samuel for two reasons: He believed, encouraged by Trever, that he could sell the scrolls for a great deal of money in the United States; also, in possessing antiquities purchased from black-market operatives, he was in technical violation of the law. When the St. Mark's monks first brought the scrolls to ASOR, they had said that they had been in the library of St. Mark's for forty years, years before the British Mandate and its antiquities laws. Weeks later, they reluctantly told ASOR that they had been acquired less than a year previously and had been found by Bedouin in the Judean desert.

Throughout March 1948 the ASOR team tried to locate people who could take them to the cave. Turning the archbishop in was the farthest thing from their collective mind. Manuscripts found in an old monastery were exciting—but manuscripts found in an identifiable archaeological context were even more significant. Archaeologists can tell a great deal about the date and origin of artifacts if their original find-spot is known. But it was too late for cave-hunting. Jewish forces controlled the approaches to the Judean desert; besides, those who knew the cave's location (the Bedouin, Kando, George Isaiah, and a few others) were in no hurry to jeopardize themselves by coming forward and confessing. Not only that, but there were still objects in the cave worth some money. Telling the authorities about them would cut off a profitable source of income.

At any rate, all agreed that the scrolls had to be moved. On March 25, Fr. Butrus Sowmy and the archbishop took them to Beirut. Within ten days, Burrows, Brownlee, and Trever (tenderly carrying the scroll negatives) departed for the States. "Thus," wrote Sukenik bitterly in his journal, "the Jewish people have lost a precious heritage." He died in 1953, while the archbishop still held the scrolls.

"An Ideal Gift"

The four St. Mark's scrolls remained in Beirut throughout 1948. After the British left Palestine, the Israelis fought off the Arab forces and established a Jewish state west of the Jordan river. In January of 1949, Mar Samuel, encouraged by the Patriarch of his church, traveled to the States with the four St. Mark's scrolls to seek contributions for the support of Palestinian refugees of the Syrian Orthodox church and for the repair of St. Mark's, which had been damaged by shellfire. One way the archbishop hoped to raise money was by selling the scrolls.

From 1949 to 1951, the scrolls were displayed at several museums and art galleries on the East Coast. Public interest was keen, but no buyers were found. Some scholars stated that the scrolls were a fraud. Sukenik publicly claimed that the scrolls belonged to the state of Israel, while the Kingdom of Jordan—which at that time included the Judean wilderness—also claimed title to the scrolls. (Neither state existed, of course, at the time of discovery!) Furthermore, Anton Kiraz, the archbishop's one-time partner, had emerged. Having been swept away in the sea of Palestinian refugees after the 1948 war, he now came forward to claim a half interest in any profit made from the scrolls. Add to the list the archbishop's rumored asking price of one million dollars, and it is no wonder no buyers came forward.

Finally, in 1954, the archbishop was reduced to putting an ad in the *Wall Street Journal:* "Biblical manuscripts dating back to at least 200 B.C. are for sale. This would be an ideal gift to an educational or religious institution by an individual or group." As luck would have it, Sukenik's son, Yigael Yadin, was in the States at the time. When he saw the ad, he immediately took steps to buy the scrolls on behalf of the state of Israel. Since Yadin and his advisors—one of whom was Albright—deemed it unlikely that the archbishop would knowingly sell the scrolls to Israel, Yadin, an old hand at covert operations, set up a number of incognito intermediaries to contact Mar Samuel and to carry out the deal. The manuscript expert chosen to examine the merchandise was Prof. Harry Orlinksy of Hebrew Union College, New York. His narrative reads like a passage from a spy novel:

> I was to assume the name "Mr. Green," an expert on behalf of the client. I was to take a taxi to the Lexington Avenue entrance of the Waldorf-Astoria Hotel, where the Chemical Bank and Trust Co. had a branch. I was to make sure that I was not followed. A Mr. Sydney M. Estridge would be waiting there for me; we had been told how to identify one another. He would go with me downstairs to the vault of the bank. There we would find a representative of the Metropolitan, with the scrolls ready for examination. I was to say as little as possible, and admit to no identification beyond being Mr. Green. . . . After leaving the vault, I phoned an unlisted number and spoke the word "*lechayim,*" meaning the scrolls were genuine.[11]

By February 1955, the scrolls were safely in Israel. The archbishop read, to his surprise, that his anonymous purchasers, who had paid $250,000,[12] were representatives of the State of Israel. The Kingdom of Jordan could not sue for possession of the scrolls without recognizing the state of Israel as a legal entity. This it refused to do. The seven original scrolls were reunited at last.

The archbishop professed in *Treasure of Qumran* that he was satisfied with the final resting place of the scrolls. But in a 1991 interview with the *Boston Globe,* the truth came out. "I wanted the scrolls to stay in America; I never knew they would go to Israel," he confessed. "Now I'm sorry I sold them."[13]

Trever had passionately hoped that the scrolls could be returned to Jordan. "Another battle of the scrolls was ended," he wrote later, bitter in his turn. "Dr. Sukenik had won, posthumously. I had lost."[14]

The Cave One Scrolls

At this point it is appropriate to describe these seven original Dead Sea Scrolls more fully and to explain why they were, and continue to be, considered so important.

To the first scholars the most exciting of the scrolls was the Isaiah scroll. Even now, after the discovery of ten more caves containing manuscripts, the St. Mark's Isaiah scroll is still the finest physical specimen of all the scrolls. And, although older biblical manuscripts have been found in the caves of the Judean desert, the Isaiah scroll is the oldest complete manuscript of a biblical book. To understand the significance of this, a short history lesson is in order.

Due to the perishability of the materials scribes wrote on

(papyrus or leather), most of the ancient literature that has survived to our day has done so only in fairly recent copies. For instance, there are about 150 surviving manuscripts of the Greek poet Aeschylus of the fifth century B.C.; almost all of them date from the fourteenth century A.D. or later. The same is true of existing manuscripts of the Old and New Testaments. Manuscripts for the New Testament are far more numerous, over five thousand, and a few of these go back to the third century A.D. Compared with the rest of Greco-Roman literature, this is extraordinarily abundant manuscript evidence.

But the Old Testament, before the Dead Sea Scrolls, existed only in more recent copies. The oldest complete manuscripts dated from between the sixth and tenth centuries A.D. Most had been copied by the Jewish scribal guild known as the Masoretes, and the text contained in their copies is called the Masoretic text. Each copy of the Masoretic text differs only slightly from the others, because the Masoretes strived for pinpoint accuracy in scribal practice. They succeeded in fixing the most stable text possible before the age of printing. But before 1947 the oldest Hebrew manuscript known, and the only ancient non-Masoretic one, was the short Nash papyrus fragment from the first century B.C. mentioned earlier.

Hence, from the modern historian's standpoint, almost every ancient book, including the Bible, enters a kind of evidential limbo at the time of its composition and only emerges to be seen, in manuscripts, in relatively recent times. What happens to it in that tunnel—that period not attested by surviving manuscripts—is open to speculation.

The shorter the tunnel, the better; the farther back the manuscripts go, the more readily scholars can track the history of copying, compare manuscripts, figure out when, where, how, and if scribal errors or intentional alterations were made, and thus arrive at a sound basis for reading and translation of the ancient author. This process is called textual criticism. The tunnel period of the New Testament is relatively short. With the Old Testament, the tunnel was fairly long, until the discovery of the Dead Sea Scrolls.

The St. Mark's Isaiah scroll is now dated to the late second or early first century B.C. The prophet Isaiah lived in the eighth century B.C. Hence the Isaiah scroll does not by any means take us back to the period of the original autograph; but, at a stroke, it brings the text of Isaiah up out of the tunnel a good millennium before the earliest Masoretic manuscript. It is no wonder neither Sukenik nor Trever could sleep after realizing what the scroll was.

The first scholars to study the scroll quickly realized that, although the text differed in certain details from the Masoretic Isaiah—especially in the spelling of the Hebrew—, it was substantially the very same biblical text. This confirmed the general reliability of the transmission of the Masoretic text throughout much of the tunnel period—a reliability that scholars were gratified to have confirmed at such an early date.[15]

There was another copy of Isaiah among the original seven scrolls, the third one Sukenik acquired. It was in poor condition—the leather was brittle, not supple, and difficult to unroll—and parts of the scroll were missing or in fragments. Yet this scroll's text proved to be even closer to the Masoretic text of Isaiah than the St. Mark's scroll, even to the details of spelling.

The five remaining scrolls were not copies of biblical books, although one of them was a commentary on the prophet Habakkuk. They were books that had previously been unknown. Scholars have given them the following names:

1. The *Manual of Discipline*[16] is a collection of rules and regulations for the ordering of a Jewish religious commune, along with some psalms and theological instruction. It consists of eleven columns of text. Seven additional columns were discovered in further excavations of Cave 1 in 1949, containing two further compositions, the *Rule of the Congregation* and the *Words of Blessing*.

2. The *War Scroll*, or the *Rule of War*, is also a collection of rules, regulations, and hymns, but has to do with the holy war of the "Sons of Light"—who may be the members of the commune described in the *Manual of Discipline*—against the "Sons of Darkness" in the last days. Its nineteen columns contain almost the complete work, although the lower edge is badly damaged, and a final column is only partially preserved.

3. The *Thanksgiving Scroll* contains about twenty psalms of thanksgiving and praise written in biblical phraseology but not corresponding to any biblical psalms. Parts at the beginning and end of the scroll are missing; eighteen columns are at least partly legible. It was a fragment from this scroll that was shown Sukenik at the meeting by the barbed wire fence.

4. The *Commentary on Habakkuk* is a verse-by-verse commentary, interpreting the prophetic message as being fulfilled in certain historic events that probably relate to the life of the same communal sect described in the *Manual of Discipline*. The historical references are obscure, because the author uses symbolic or "code" names to refer to the figures and events described. This scroll of eleven columns—incomplete due to the loss of the first few columns and the lower lines—is usually known today as the *Habakkuk Pesher,* after the Hebrew word for interpretation or secret meaning that is used so often in it.

5. The last scroll of the original lot lay unopened until 1956. It was in the poorest condition of them all, parts of the leather having decomposed into a solid lump; the pages that remained intact were stuck tightly together, and the whole scroll was blackened by age and badly eaten away. After Israel acquired the scroll, experts opened it to find an Aramaic retelling of the book of Genesis, told from the perspective of the characters. It was named the *Genesis Apocryphon*. (In this context, *apocryphon* [plural *apocrypha*] refers to a noncanonical version of Scriptural stories.) Only three complete columns are readable, of a total of twenty-two, and only portions of the rest. Work still continues today on this scroll, as scientists try different methods to bring out the text on the damaged portions of the scroll.

These, then, were the original seven Dead Sea Scrolls. One more writing needs to be mentioned alongside them, a document from medieval times that came to be included early on with the original seven as a kind of "honorary" Dead Sea Scroll—honorary, that is, until fragments of ancient copies were discovered in other Dead Sea caves. The text is known today as the *Damascus Document* or the *Damascus Rule*.

The *Damascus Document* is known to us from a significant manuscript discovery made in 1895, that of the Cairo Geniza. A geniza is a storeroom in a synagogue for worn-out or defective manuscripts. A geniza dating back to the Middle Ages was discovered in Cairo containing over twenty thousand manuscripts from as early as the sixth century A.D. Two of the geniza manuscripts were partial copies of the *Damascus Document,* which is similar to the *Manual of Discipline* in giving rules for a Jewish sect said to live in Damascus; it also contains a number of historical

Figure 1

allusions to the same obscure characters mentioned in the *Habakkuk Pesher*.

Initially these seven scrolls were roughly dated to the second or first centuries B.C. on the basis of paleography. Paleographers study the shape of letters and their evolution. Figure 1 illustrates the evolution of the Hebrew/Aramaic letter *samekh,* equivalent to the English *S*. It begins as a "telephone pole" (1), evolves into a "zigzag on a stick" (2), then starts to develop more cursive forms (3, 4). It gradually starts to look something like a bent nail (5, 6). Finally its "head" lengthens, almost reaching the "foot" (7), and reaches its final stage as a closed figure (8), as it still is today (9). The earliest scrolls have forms like 6, but most vary between the "open samekh"

(7) and the "closed samekh" (8). The "open samekh" is an earlier form; but paleographers insist on finding a majority of such earlier forms before they date an entire scroll early. By taking into account all the letter forms, paleographers today believe they can date a scroll to within twenty-five to forty years.

Today the Cave 1 scrolls are on permanent display in the elegant "Shrine of the Book" in Jerusalem.

Notes

1. Weston W. Fields, "The Shepherd Boy Who Discovered the Scrolls" (Jerusalem: Dead Sea Scrolls Foundation, 1993). The variety of stories seems to originate with Muhammad and the other Bedouin who were involved, who either didn't remember clearly what had happened, or who may have amused themselves by telling a different tale to every earnest Westerner who asked them. There are a number of stories that deny the discovery of the first scrolls in Cave 1 altogether and place their origin in the looting of a Hebrew synagogue in the twenties, or, according to a dark rumor heard by William Brownlee in the early sixties, the scrolls were found in 1938, and murder was committed to acquire them (*Revue de Qumran* 3 [1961-62], 493 n. 28).

2. Fields, "Shepherd Boy."

3. His autobiography, *Treasure of Qumran: My Story of the Dead Sea Scrolls* (Philadelphia: Westminster, 1966), is a rather florid defense of his own rectitude.

4. Edmund Wilson, *Israel and the Dead Sea Scrolls* (New York: Farrar Straus Giroux, 1978), 118.

5. Yigael Yadin, *The Message of the Scrolls* (New York: Simon & Schuster, 1957), 17–18.

6. In fact, Samuel's activities between September and January are somewhat mysterious. Apparently he left Palestine for Syria at some point seeking interested buyers, but without result. It is also unclear at what point Kiraz entered the picture, and it is possible he had advised Samuel from the beginning. Kiraz later claimed that the archbishop promised him a half-interest in any proceeds from the sale of the scrolls. Detailed discussions of these episodes can be found in John C. Trever's *Untold Story of Qumran* (Westwood, N.J.: Revell, 1965), 108–13, and Samuel's *Treasure of Qumran*, 152–56.

7. Samuel, *Treasure of Qumran*, 156.

8. Trever, "The Discovery of the Scrolls," *Biblical Archaeologist* 11 (1948): 50.

9. See Philip J. King, *American Archaeology in the Mideast: A History of the American Schools of Oriental Research* (Philadelphia: ASOR, 1983), 109.

10. For instance, he refers, apparently without irony, to "the Jewish problem" (15). He comes close to blaming Jews for anti-Semitism: "Anti-

seeking interested buyers, but without result. It is also unclear at what point Kiraz entered the picture, and it is possible he had advised Samuel from the beginning. Kiraz later claimed that the archbishop promised him a half-interest in any proceeds from the sale of the scrolls. Detailed discussions of these episodes can be found in John C. Trever's *Untold Story of Qumran* (Westwood, N.J.: Revell, 1965), 108–13, and Samuel's *Treasure of Qumran,* 152–56.

7. Samuel, *Treasure of Qumran,* 156.

8. Trever, "The Discovery of the Scrolls," *Biblical Archaeologist* 11 (1948): 50.

9. See Philip J. King, *American Archaeology in the Mideast: A History of the American Schools of Oriental Research* (Philadelphia: ASOR, 1983), 109.

10. For instance, he refers, apparently without irony, to "the Jewish problem" (15). He comes close to blaming Jews for anti-Semitism: "Anti-Semitism is a shameful stain on Christian civilization, but it can be eradicated if the Jews themselves will do their part" (86). The quotations are from *Palestine Is Our Business* (Philadelphia: Westminster, 1949).

11. Harry Orlinksy, "The Mysterious Mr. Green," *Reform Judaism* 20/3 (Spring 1992): 47–48.

12. More than a third of the archbishop's money would be paid to the government as capital gains tax.

13. *Boston Globe,* 2 October 1991, 26.

14. Trever, *Untold Story,* 143.

15. In fact, prior to the discovery of the scrolls, textual critics were already tending to see the Masoretic text as more reliable than had previous critics. Research in ancient languages related to Hebrew, such as Ugaritic and Akkadian, convinced many that the Masoretes had preserved authentically ancient linguistic forms in the Old Testament. Thus in 1938 D. Winton Thomas could already speak of "the restoration of the reputation of the Masoretic text"; see his "Language of the Old Testament," in H. W. Robinson, ed., *Record and Revelation* (New York: Oxford University Press, 1938), 401.

16. Burrows gave the name *Manual of Discipline* to the scroll (initially known as the "Sectarian Document") because it reminded him vaguely of the Methodist *Manual of Discipline,* which he had in fact never read (Burrows, *The Dead Sea Scrolls* [New York: Viking, 1955], 24). If Burrows had used the terminology of his own denomination (Presbyterian), the scroll might be known today by the more suitable name of *The Book of Order.*

Chapter 2

More Caves, More Scrolls—and Controversy

After returning to the States, the ASOR team of Burrows, Trever, and Brownlee quickly began to publicize their find in scholarly journals and, in 1950, by the publication of Trever's photos of the St. Mark's Isaiah scroll and the *Habakkuk Pesher*. In 1951, Brownlee published the *Manual of Discipline*. Worldwide scholarly interest was intense and immediate. Since ASOR had taken the unusual step of publishing their texts without any interpretive comments, aside from a transcription into modern Hebrew characters, many scholars were eager to provide translations, commentary, and interpretation.

Sukenik published portions of his scrolls as early as 1948; all were published in a single volume in 1955, in a spare format similar to ASOR's. Thus all the scrolls, except for the *Genesis Apocryphon* (published in 1956), were available within seven years of their discovery.

Some scholars were excited about the Dead Sea Scrolls for a different reason—they believed them to be a hoax. Foremost among them was Prof. Solomon Zeitlin of Dropsie College in Philadelphia. Zeitlin was a noted authority on intertestamental Judaism and Jewish law. He immediately decided that the scrolls were fraudulent. "I have never had any doubt whatsoever in my mind that these scrolls were not of the pre-Christian period," he wrote.[1] In a series of articles in the *Jewish Quarterly Review,* of which he was editor, he denied the validity of the paleographical dating, stressed the lack of archaeological context, asserted that several expressions used in the scrolls were typical of medieval texts, emphasized the suspicious nature of the transactions by which the scrolls were obtained, and suggested the complicity of the archbishop in an elaborate conspiracy. He said that the manuscripts were "the work of mediocre persons"[2] and that the ASOR team and Sukenik were fools "to rely on the word of a goatherd."[3]

At a remove of several decades, it is fascinating to re-read Zeitlin's articles and observe that, as the evidence against his views piles up, Zeitlin's unruliness increases rather than slackens. His strident articles bore titles like "The Fiction of the Recent Discoveries Near the Dead Sea," "The Antiquity of the Hebrew Scrolls and the Piltdown Hoax: A Parallel," "The Propaganda of the Hebrew Scrolls and the Falsification of History," and so on. The role of skeptic is an important one, of course, particularly with a discovery so fraught with significance as the Dead Sea Scrolls. Yet Zeitlin in retrospect gives the impression of a man who is not only not convinced, but refuses to be convinced. He could not understand the methods being used, and he retreated behind a wall of disdain.

There is some evidence that Zeitlin was irritated by the magisterial way Albright delivered his opinions on the scrolls. The letter to Trever, quoted earlier, is an example: "there happily cannot be the slightest doubt about the genuineness of the find." Well, actually, there could be, and Zeitlin expressed them, again and again. This early conflict, which has been called the first "battle of the scrolls," quickly became a fight for supremacy between Albright and Zeitlin and their proxies. It got nasty at times. In 1950, Albright wrote, "How any man who claims the name 'scholar' can fail to recognize the tremendous importance of the Scrolls in the light of the rapidly accumulating evidence is extremely hard to see."[4] The hyperbolic rhetoric—*tremendous, rapidly, extremely*—is pure Albright. In reply, Zeitlin raged against Albright's "*ex cathedra* pronouncements."

Part of the difficulty was that the two men simply spoke different academic languages. Albright was most at home in archaeology, Zeitlin in Jewish history. Ideally, the two disciplines would complement each other; in this case, neither man could communicate in the other's terms or address the other's concerns, and didn't desire to. When it came down to a literal one-on-one debate in Philadelphia, one of Albright's Jewish students gave him this advice:

> "Don't get entangled with Zeitlin in Talmudic jurisprudence because it will entrap you and you will not get out of it. Just speak in the terms and in the literature that you know best, and leave him to speak about the Talmudic evidence, and you disregard it!" . . . [Albright] always reminded me afterward that this was very good advice, because he gave a fine address and really defeated Zeitlin. The audience clapped and applauded him tremendously.[5]

Ultimately Albright's point of view prevailed, primarily because the vital points at issue—the external evidence for or against the dating of the scrolls—fell within his specialty, and not within Zeitlin's.

This first "battle of the scrolls" no doubt contributed to the bear market for manuscripts that Archbishop Samuel confronted during this period. But after a certain point, Zeitlin found himself virtually ignored. Although he continued to publish his critiques of Dead Sea Scrolls scholarship, specialists, satisfied that the scrolls were truly ancient, moved past him to other questions. Millar Burrows, one of the participants in this battle, wrote two books on the Dead Sea Scrolls, bestsellers in their day: *The Dead Sea Scrolls* (1955) and *More Light on the Dead Sea Scrolls* (1958). In the first, Zeitlin's name is mentioned more than seventeen times; in the second, not even once.[6]

The Authorities Take Over

While scholars wrangled over the dating and authenticity of the scrolls, the Holy Land had become, if not calm, at least stable. The 1948 boundary line between the new states of Israel and Jordan left East Jerusalem—including the Old City, the ASOR building, and the Palestine Archaeological Museum—on the Jordanian side, as was the Wilderness of Judah. It will be recalled that the ASOR team, before they left, was anxious to locate the "manuscript cave," but was unable to mount a search. After the cessation of hostilities, a different set of scholars had the same ambition.

One of them was G. Lankester Harding, who had been director of the Antiquities Department under the British Mandate and who kept the same post under the Jordanian government. He had not even heard of the discovery until he read an article by Albright in an American journal. Furious that there had been a momentous discovery right under his nose—and that antiquities had been illegally bought, sold, and removed from the country—he determined to bring the entire business under his jurisdiction. That meant finding the cave and those who had looted it.

Harding found this task harder than expected. George Isaiah, whom Harding had traced as a middleman, refused to talk. Harding and others tried a number of dubious strategems to find the cave, including hiring two Taamireh Bedouin who had served in the army to infiltrate their nomadic brethren and to find out what they could, which turned out to be nothing. Finally, Harding decided to bypass the original discoverers altogether. He received permission for the soldiers of the Arab Legion, the crack Jordanian military unit, to comb the general area where the cave was thought to be located.

On January 28, 1949, a captain of the Legion noticed that the dirt in front of one hole had been disturbed. Climbing up, he saw that a copious amount of dirt from inside the cave had been thrown out, apparently in the course of a thorough ransacking. He had found the manuscript cave.

Harding lost no time. From February to March 1949, he subjected the cave to a comprehensive examination, aided by Father Roland de Vaux, an archaeologist with L'École Biblique et Archéologique Française, an institution founded in 1890 by French Dominican monks for biblical and archaeological study in the Holy Land. Harding and de Vaux made important discoveries—most notably, fragments of scrolls, including more bits of the scrolls already known. This confirmed that the cave was the very cave from which the original scrolls were taken. They also found many potsherds, the most common artifact in any excavation. Some of the pottery appeared to date from the Roman period (after A.D. 70), but the vast majority came from pre-Christian times, supporting earlier guesses as to the general period the manuscripts were written.

Still, even with these results, Harding and de Vaux were disgusted at the state the cave was left in. Cigarette butts, newspapers, and other twentieth-century garbage betrayed the fact that, after the initial find, more Bedouin and probably monks from St. Mark's had made subsequent searches in the cave. Harding was sure that other scrolls had been found and secretly stashed away. He still had no idea where they were or who had them.

It took over a year for Harding and his assistants to trace the dealer Kando and convince him that, far from contemplating legal action against him, they wished to buy whatever scrolls he had gotten from his Bedouin clients as well as any ancient inscribed material he might receive in the future. Kando agreed and promptly (for 1000 pounds!) handed over a large pile of scroll fragments taken from the cave.

This partnership between the authorities and the unofficial antiquities trade seems odd, not to say shady, but Harding had no choice. The Bedouin and Kando had the scrolls. If Harding had jailed the lawbreakers, the scrolls would have been sold to private collectors or possibly just thrown away. As it was, while Harding was searching for Kando, the dealer had taken fright and buried one scroll in his backyard. When it was found later, it had completely disintegrated. To avoid any further loss, Harding agreed to become Kando's major customer.

The system was open to abuse, and in fact was abused. Harding had no guarantee that Kando would actually pass on to him all of the Bedouin finds—later evidence showed he clearly did not. But the immediate effect of legitimizing scroll trafficking was the discovery of more caves containing yet more scrolls. In October 1951, Bedouin found manuscripts from four caves south of Bethlehem, in the Wadi Murabbaat.[7] Though the scrolls proved to be from a time a century or more later than the first Dead Sea Scrolls found near the Wadi Qumran, they were still important, and encouraged the searchers to persevere in combing the region.

Besides searching caves, de Vaux and Harding began investigating an ancient ruin near the caves called Khirbet Qumran (Arabic for "ruins of Qumran"), situated on a cliff near the debouch of the wadi into the Dead Sea valley. The archaeologists guessed that the "library" of the first cave had belonged to a specific group living in the area in ancient times. Their first thought was to look near Ain Feshkha, a nearby oasis close to the shore of the Dead Sea, but at the time they saw no trace of ancient habitation. (Minor ruins were discovered there in 1958.) Their next guess was to look at Khirbet Qumran. Work began there in November 1951 and continued, at intervals, until 1956. De Vaux concluded, on the basis of the potsherds, writing apparatus, and other evidence, that Khirbet Qumran was indeed the ancient center of the group responsible for the scrolls. Since, in de Vaux's estimation, the buildings ceased to be inhabited in A.D. 68, the scrolls had to have been written by that time.

In February 1952, the Bedouin found a second cave containing scroll fragments in the Qumran area. Though the manuscripts were far fewer in number than the first cave, the find spurred Western scholars to attempt their own search. By the end of March, teams from ASOR had investigated more than two hundred caves, holes, and crevices near the Wadi Qumran, with one payoff: the discovery of Cave 3. From it scholars removed not only a few dozen leather scroll fragments, but one intact document, the *Copper Scroll*. This remarkable text—written in Hebrew letters punched into a long copper sheet—remained unread until 1956 because the copper had rusted into a stiff unrollable cylinder. To this day, it is the only major scroll that Westerners have found in its original location.

The Main Lode

In September 1952, de Vaux bought for the Antiquities Department a huge pile of fragments, evidently from a fourth cave, which proved to be the "main lode,"[8] yielding, in the end, remains of hundreds of manuscripts. Westerners finally located Cave 4 only a few hundred feet from Khirbet Qumran itself. Taamireh tribesmen had already pulled out over three-quarters of the fragments, but a massive amount still remained—the richest find of all, but in poor condition. All of the texts had been in pieces since ancient times, and were covered by the dust of centuries and buried under a deep layer of bat dung. It would take years to put the scraps in any kind of order.

It was the biggest find, but not the last. Excavators working on Cave 4 found Cave 5 days later in the same vicinity, then Cave 6, containing fragments of the *Damascus Document*. Caves 7–10 followed in 1955, but they contained only a few scraps in all. Finally, in 1956, Bedouin sold to Kando at least seven well-preserved scrolls from Cave 11—the first manuscripts to be preserved in so complete a form since the discovery of Cave 1.

Although the importance of these finds was immeasurable, the funds available to Harding, the Jordan Department of Antiquities, and the Palestine Archaeological Museum were not. Though the museum, an internationally administered entity with its own endowment, was independent of the Jordanian government, the Dead Sea Scrolls brought them together. The Jordanian Amman Museum was not equipped to handle the material, but the Palestine Museum could not afford to buy the material. To keep the scrolls in Jordan, the government donated money to the museum to buy the scrolls from the Bedouin.

But by the time Cave 4 was discovered, Harding's arrangement with Kando had bled the government of all available funds, with hundreds of valuable scroll fragments still in the hands of Kando and the Bedouin. A reluctant call for monetary help went out to international foundations and universities asking for contributions to fund further scroll purchases. Harding promised donors that once the material had been scientifically studied and published, the scroll fragments would be handed over to the funding institutions. Money began to pour in, not only from universities and seminaries, but also from the Vatican and the West German government. By 1956 the majority of the Cave 4 material was in the hands of the authorities, though Kando was still selling oddments from the find to private buyers as late as 1958.

The Cave 11 scrolls caused another problem. In early 1956, when Kando brought the scrolls to the museum, Jordan was deeply involved in the Suez crisis. Bitter anti-Western feeling ultimately led to the dismissal of Harding, and a rift then developed between the government and the Western-dominated museum, which could no longer count on official help in soliciting funds.

Finally the trustees cashed in a large part of its endowment to buy as many scrolls as it could, then, to recoup its losses, virtually auctioned each scroll to the highest bidder for publication rights. The Royal Dutch Academy bought an incomplete scroll containing an Aramaic translation of the Book of Job, as well as fragments of other texts; ASOR, having received a large donation from American philanthropist Elizabeth Hays Bechtel, got the rights to other scrolls, including a beautifully preserved manuscript of part of the

Book of Psalms. But Kando held back the prize discovery of Cave 11, the *Temple Scroll,* the longest of all the Dead Sea Scrolls (its fate is discussed in chapter 3). Rumors persist that private collectors or other unknown agencies possess still more Cave 11 material.

The Cave 4 Team

The unexpected avalanche of scrolls and fragments that came pouring out of the eleven Qumran caves caused financial problems for the authorities, as we have seen, but it also caused a different sort of problem for Harding.

The new scrolls that were finding their way to the museum were in pieces, most of them quite small. It is estimated that the entire collection of Cave 4 texts numbers around 15,000 fragments. Obviously, a book of photos of such bits and pieces would be of little use. People had to be found who knew Hebrew and Aramaic, were familiar with the ancient script, and had the time to piece together scrolls out of tiny fragments.

Since there were no Jordanian scholars with such qualifications, Harding asked the international archaeological societies that resided in Jordan to suggest names of qualified specialists who could come to East Jerusalem and work on the scrolls. During the years 1953 and 1954, Harding assembled in East Jerusalem eight young academics nominated from the different countries: from the United States, Frank Moore Cross of McCormick Theological Seminary (later of Harvard) and Patrick Skehan of the Catholic University of America; from France, Dominique Barthélemy and Jean Starcky; from Poland, J. T. Milik; from Great Britain, two young graduate students, John Allegro of Manchester University and John Strugnell of Oxford; and from West Germany, Claus Hunzinger. Four were Catholic priests, three were Protestants, and one—Allegro—was an atheist. Later, another French priest, Maurice Baillet, was added to work on the meager finds from the "minor" caves. Roland de Vaux, president of the museum board of trustees, was chosen to direct the team.

De Vaux has been portrayed as an autocratic villain who packed the international team with "a small coterie of his closest colleagues."[9] Whatever may have been de Vaux's personal characteristics—everyone agrees he had a robust ego—he was not responsible for picking the team members. The initial idea came from Harding; the actual nominations were made by prominent biblical scholars from the several nations involved.[10]

Harding and de Vaux wanted a team that would truly represent the nations and creeds that were active in biblical scholarship, with one major exception: They could not include any Jews or Israelis. It has been argued that de Vaux himself was anti-Semitic; it is certain that, like Burrows, Trever, and many other scholars, he was vehemently opposed to the establishment of the state of Israel. But since he was acting on behalf of the Jordanian government, de Vaux could not have included Jews or Israelis on his team even if he had wanted to. In the fifties, even Albright was banned from traveling in Arab countries due to his friendliness with Israelis. De Vaux kept up a regular correspondence with Yadin (an Israeli general!), but had to send his letters from East Jerusalem to a mutual friend in Paris who would forward them to Yadin in West Jerusalem.[11]

With these limitations, then, in 1953 the group began to trickle into Jerusalem. These men formed the core of what was later called the "scrolls cartel." No one at the time could have anticipated such a negative description; the purpose of the team was not to keep the scrolls secret, but to make sure they were published as quickly as possible.

Much work had to be done. The Cave 4 texts were in much worse shape than the Cave 1 scrolls. They had not been stored in jars, but were left in the dirt, where worms and ants had been at them for centuries. Some of them were so blackened by age that they had to be photographed first under infrared light before any writing became visible. Others had been wadded up or cut into pieces in ancient times. All were extremely fragile.

A large room in the Palestine Museum was set up for the team. The "Scrollery" had long tables that allowed the team to sort through the thousands of leather scraps, joining fragment to fragment when possible. When a scholar had restored as much as possible of a particular scroll—often only half a column, or perhaps a dozen disconnected paragraphs—the fragile leather was placed between sheets of glass and photographed.[12]

Although the men had to read the texts in order to join piece to piece, the real work of translation and interpretation could not begin until the tedious reconstruction was complete. By 1956, the team had finished putting together much of the Cave 4 material.[13] Although Kando and the Bedouin still had some choice pieces, the team was ready to begin transcribing and translating a majority of the Cave 4 texts.

The year 1956 was significant for the study of the Dead Sea Scrolls, or Qumran studies, as it was beginning to be called. The *Genesis Apocryphon* from Cave 1 and the *Copper Scroll* from Cave 3 were unrolled and read, and public interest had put several books about the scrolls on the best-seller list. The Bedouin discovered new manuscripts in Cave 11. And the Cave 4 team added to all the excitement by collaborating on a progress report of their work and describing which texts had been given to whom to publish.[14]

It was a rich collection that the Cave 4 team described for the learned world. Old Testament texts were present in the collection in profusion: not only texts resembling the Masoretic text, as with the great Isaiah scroll, but also texts that differed from the Masoretic text and agreed with the Septuagint, the Greek translation of the Old Testament from the third century B.C. Other biblical texts showed variations from both the Masoretic and Septuagint types.[15]

Besides the abundance of Old Testament manuscripts, Cave 4 also offered Hebrew and Aramaic originals of some ancient Jewish books that had long been known only in later translations into Greek or other languages, such as *The Book of Tobit* (part of the Apocrypha, a collection of writings included in the canon of Scripture in some Christian traditions, but often excluded by others, especially evangelical Protestants), *The Book of Jubilees* (an ancient rewriting of Genesis, with legendary material), and *The Book of Enoch* (a long collection of stories and visions about the biblical Enoch and purporting to be by him).

Documents were found that were nothing like those previously known. Pieces of the *War Scroll*, the *Manual of Discipline*, the *Damascus Document* (including sections not known from the later medieval copy), turned up, but lots of other interesting items as well—commentaries in the enigmatic style of the *Habakkuk Pesher*, but this time on Nahum, on Psalms, on Genesis, and others, as well as fragments of poetry, hymns, sermons, occult astrological literature, scraps written in code, and texts dealing with calendars and Jewish religious law. All of these promised to revolutionize the study of the Bible and to cast much light on the history of Judaism and Christianity.

Each member of the team took responsibility for a certain number of manuscripts, according to the type of material. Cross and Skehan assumed the task of preparing many of the Old Testament manuscripts for publication. J. T. Milik's allotment of manuscripts included many of the most interesting nonbiblical and sectarian texts. The responsibility for many fragments written in Aramaic fell to Jean Starcky, an expert in ancient Aramaic inscriptions. Allegro and Strugnell took on a number of commentaries, poetic works, and legal texts. Germany's C. H. Hunzinger decided to work on the fragments of the *War Scroll,* while Baillet busied himself with the fragments from the other caves.[16]

De Vaux's plan was to publish the texts in an elaborate format. Each volume of a series of books called *Discoveries in the Judean Desert* (*DJD*) would be devoted to one scholar's allotment and would contain not only photos and transcription, but extensive commentary placing the texts in historical, literary, and linguistic context.

Several team members went ahead and published "preliminary editions" of particularly interesting or significant fragments, without waiting for their appearance in *DJD*. Cross, Milik, and Allegro published successful books for a popular audience describing their work and the significance of the scrolls.[17] The work of the team seemed to have gotten off to a good start.

The Dead Sea Scrolls were frequently in the news at this time. In the United States, public interest in the finds was widespread. Dozens of books were published for the general public between 1955 and 1958 detailing the significance of the finds and explaining their implications for biblical study.[18] But as the fifties drew to a close with no more sensational new developments, only specialists in history, language, and biblical studies continued to be interested.

But more than thirty years later the Dead Sea Scrolls would explode into the headlines again, acquainting a new generation with their power to fascinate, excite, and, just possibly, to confuse. That narrative will occupy another chapter. But looking back on the story of the original discovery, let us note how the Dead Sea Scrolls were from the beginning accompanied by avarice, ego, and prejudice, as well as courage, curiosity, and the thirst for knowledge. Is it any wonder that the characters in the sequel should be animated by the same passions?

Notes

1. "The Alleged Antiquity of the Scrolls," *Jewish Quarterly Review* 40 (1949–50): 57.

2. Ibid., 72.

3. "When Were the Hebrew Scrolls 'Discovered'–in 1947 or 1907?" *Jewish Quarterly Review* 40 (1949–50): 376.

4. Quoted in S. Zeitlin, "The Hebrew Scrolls: A Challenge to Scholarship," *Jewish Quarterly Review* 41 (1950–51): 275.

5. Samuel Iwry, quoted in L. G. Running and David Noel Freedman, *William Foxwell Albright: A Twentieth-Century Genius* (New York: Morgan Press, 1975), 262.

6. Some fair-minded reader is bound to ask the question, "Could Zeitlin have been right? Is it not possible that scholars simply jumped on Albright's bandwagon and neglected to consider vital evidence that pointed to a hoax or at least to a medieval date for the scrolls?" There is a tiny chance that Zeitlin was right if the following scenario can be accepted:

A group of Bedouin, in collusion with the archbishop, pretend to discover certain manuscripts (which may be forgeries, or products of the Middle Ages), which they attempt to sell for a large sum of money. Having successfully fooled a huge number of gullible experts, they then hide additional bogus manuscripts in eleven caves in the Dead Sea area, some of which they help additional experts to find, some of which the experts unaccountably find for themselves. For some reason, the vast majority of archaeologists and paleographers examining these objects become convinced that they are indeed from the pre-Christian era (precisely as the conspirators hoped), a dating luckily and inexplicably confirmed by two separate radiocarbon tests. Despite forty years of intense study of the manuscripts, the wool still remains over the eyes of the learned world, while the now aging and still unidentified conspirators laugh all the way to the bank.

7. A *wadi* is a watercourse that is flooded with water during the rainy season, but dry the rest of the year. The Judean wilderness is crisscrossed with numerous wadis, large and small.

8. Frank Moore Cross, *The Ancient Library of Qumran and Modern Biblical Studies,* rev. ed. (Grand Rapids: Baker, 1980), 26.

9. Hershel Shanks, "What Should Be Done About the Unpublished Dead Sea Scrolls?" *Biblical Archaeology Review* (September/October 1989): 18. Shanks also states that "King Hussein . . . allowed Father Roland de Vaux . . . to appoint the team of editors." King Hussein was never involved in the formation of the team, either directly or indirectly.

10. Cross's and Skehan's names were submitted by the President of ASOR, Carl Kraeling, on the recommendation of Albright. Allegro was nominated by H. H. Rowley of Manchester, Strugnell by G. R. Driver of

Oxford, and Hunzinger by Joachim Jeremias of Göttingen. Only Milik and Starcky were nominated by de Vaux.

11. Geza Vermes, "Yigael Yadin and the Manuscripts from the Judaean Desert," *Bulletin of the Anglo-Israel Archaeological Society* (1984–85): 22–23.

12. Putting the scrolls between sheets of glass is an example of good intentions gone wrong, as so often happened with this discovery. Instead of preserving the scrolls, the glass, it is now known, created a kind of "greenhouse effect" in miniature. The resultant dampness and warmth have contributed to the further deterioration of the scrolls.

13. Cross, *Ancient Library of Qumran,* 39.

14. "Le travail d'édition des manuscrits de Qumran" (The Work of Editing the Manuscripts of Qumran) appeared in the official journal of the Ecole Biblique, *Revue Biblique* 63 (1956): 49–67.

15. See the appendix, "The Old Testament in Light of the Scrolls."

16. One of the original team, Father Dominique Barthélemy, dropped out early on in the process, deeming his weak eyes not up to the exacting work of restoration and publication, although he has continued to write and publish in regard to the text of the Old Testament.

17. John Allegro, *The Dead Sea Scrolls,* 1956; Milik, *Dix ans de découvertes dans le Desért du Judah* (Ten Years of Discovery in the Desert of Judah), 1957, translated into English by Strugnell in 1959; Cross, *The Ancient Library of Qumran and Modern Biblical Studies,* 1958.

18. A good survey of all the popular literature on the scrolls from this period can be found in John Reumann's "Dead Sea Scrolls in America: A Survey of Five Years of Popular Literature," *Lutheran Quarterly* 12/2 (May 1960): 91–110.

Chapter 3

Delays and Distractions

Thirty years after the discovery of Cave 1, many of the fragments from Cave 4 and the other caves were still unpublished. One scholar, speaking for all those frustrated by the slow rate of publication, complained in 1977 that "the greatest and most valuable of all Hebrew and Aramaic manuscript discoveries is likely to become the academic scandal *par excellence* of the twentieth century."[1] Fourteen years after those words were published, little had changed, and scholars calling for a rapid release of all photographs and transcriptions of the scrolls had ceased to be merely an impatient few and had begun to be a strident crowd. Others began to engage in a certain amount of skulduggery to obtain what had become, in effect, "classified information." How had "the greatest manuscript discovery" become the "academic scandal *par excellence*"?

By June 1960 the Cave 4 team members had finished making preliminary transcriptions of the material in the Palestine Archaeological Museum. The Scrollery workroom was dismantled. Most of the fragments were put away. Some were put on display in the museum in glass cases.[2] The Cave 4 team had done much of the work necessary to begin publishing all the Cave 4 material.

But they didn't. Why not?

There are several reasons why the publication proceeded slowly. Too few scholars were working on too much material, and in producing large scale commentaries on every aspect of their texts, they were trying to do too much. There was no accountability to a schedule, a supervisor, or to the authorities on whose behalf the work was being done—the museum, their trustees, or the government. These basic flaws were magnified by other factors, personal and political.

Moreover, the material was unevenly distributed. Cross, Strugnell, and Milik had taken the lion's share of the manuscripts. Of the 574 Cave 4 manuscripts that eventually were identified (the count was 382 in 1956), Milik took control of 197, while Strugnell had over 100.[3] Cross and Skehan between them had all of the biblical manuscripts, almost a third of the whole.

The success of the enterprise, then, lay mainly in the hands of Cross, Milik, Skehan, and Strugnell. How were they able to come into such commanding positions?

The Inner Circle

Cross and Milik were the first ones on the scene. Milik had already been working on the Cave 1 fragments in Jerusalem when de Vaux and Harding formed the team, and Cross was the first to arrive (in May 1953) from overseas. During 1953 Cross and Milik made an initial division of the Cave 4 fragments between biblical and nonbiblical scrolls, Cross taking responsibility for the former.

Cross had been one of Albright's star students at Johns Hopkins and had been present when the great man had received Trever's first excited letter with its photos of the Isaiah scroll. Cross quickly showed himself to be equal to his teacher in brilliance and breadth of learning, and in the fifties and sixties he became one of the most prominent and influential Old Testament scholars in America.

Milik was a genius in his own right. Allegro considered him "perhaps the most brilliant of our little team of scroll editors. . . . He developed an extraordinary facility for reading Semitic scripts of a cursive character never before seen, and for recognizing the work of individual scribes from the tiniest fragments."[4] A story of Cross's exemplifies Milik's brilliance in decipherment:

> The three of us in Jerusalem at the time set up a competition in decipherment. We worked unsuccessfully until lunch time and strolled home busily discussing decipherment techniques, about which we knew little. After lunch two of us arrived back promptly at the museum. Abbé Milik was late. Allegro and I discussed the ethics of starting before he arrived, and, of course, proceeded without him. Some minutes later Milik arrived, drew from his pocket a photograph of the fragments, and announced that he had deciphered the script during lunch.[5]

Allegro arrived toward the end of 1953 and began work on a group of scrolls under Milik's direction. Milik and the rest, however, did not find it easy to work with Allegro; Strugnell, who arrived in July 1954, proved to be a more apt apprentice, and his reputation grew to rival Milik's. James Sanders, who was later assigned the Psalms Scroll from Cave 11, said:

> I was 32 years old when I unrolled the [Psalms] scroll, and I was told all kinds of stories. I was initiated into the fact that the Cave 4 team was largely made up of raving geniuses. They would tell about how they would meet in the museum labs, face a problem, and then discuss it at the American school later that evening and so on. It would be [J.T.] Milik who would come the next day with the solution. Milik always had a solution. He seemed to have a reputation of being a particular kind of genius; so he got all the tough stuff. And Strugnell was, I think, second in line with that kind of reputation. He got the second rank of tough stuff.[6]

But despite the obvious gifts of Cross, Milik, and Strugnell, in retrospect it is clear that too much material was concentrated in their hands. Academic publishing moves at a snail's pace. Preparing even one fragment for publication can take months; publishing hundreds is a gargantuan, time-consuming task. The team as a whole was small, and all of the team members had professional obligations above and beyond their work on the scrolls. Cross, Skehan, Allegro, and Strugnell all had teaching positions, while de Vaux, Milik, and Starcky continued to do research in other fields outside the Qumran literature.

The team was reduced when Hunzinger quit in 1958, and instead of adding a new member to the team, de Vaux gave

Hunzinger's texts to Maurice Baillet, who felt he had more than enough to do as it was. Jean Starcky showed little interest in the scrolls after the closing of the Scrollery. Before his death in 1988, he had published only one of his thirty manuscripts.

John Allegro, on the other hand, published text after text of his allotment of twenty-nine during the fifties and sixties. Despite this, he caused problems for the team. Though he maintained outwardly friendly relations with the others, he felt contempt for their religious beliefs. Already in the early fifties he had begun his lifelong—and ultimately fruitless—quest for some manuscript among the scrolls that would be the "magic bullet" to bring about the collapse of Christianity.

Allegro Agonistes

In 1956, Allegro announced on the BBC that he had found a text that described the Qumran sect as worshiping a crucified Messiah whom they expected to return in glory. Since the texts were pre-Christian, Allegro suggested that Christian beliefs about Jesus were not factual but a story taken over from a previous sect. The members of the team in Jerusalem at the time were amazed when they heard about Allegro's claims, since they knew of no such text. Writing in 1966, Skehan tells what happened next:

> Arab Jerusalem was not, ten years ago, the easiest place in the world from which to register astonishment at things being said in England. But all five of us dropped our current work for a couple of days and made the rounds of the "scrollery" of the Palestine Archaeological Museum, where the Qumran texts had been collected, to see if we could discover in them anything that could significantly support what our colleague had told his B.B.C. audience. Then we wrote a letter to the London *Times*. . . .[7]

The letter, printed in the name of de Vaux, Milik, Starcky, Skehan, and Strugnell, said: "We are unable to see in the texts the 'findings' of Mr. Allegro. . . . It is our conviction that either he has misread the texts or he has built up a chain of conjectures which the materials do not support." Allegro retracted his claims, admitting that he had stated as fact something he had read into the text. That settled matters for the moment, but Allegro's relationships with the other team members deteriorated.

Allegro created further antagonism in the controversy over the *Copper Scroll*. This was the document discovered in March 1952 in Cave 3, but proved impossible to unroll because age had made it stiff and rusty. One scholar, viewing the scroll at the Palestine Museum, tried to make out some of the contents of the scroll from the deeply embossed letters visible on the back. His opinion was that the scroll contained a description of buried treasure.

In 1956 the scroll was sent to the Manchester College of Science and Technology in England, where, instead of being unrolled, an engineer cut it into strips, being careful to make his incisions between the letters. Allegro was teaching then at the University of Manchester and was the first to read the scroll in its entirety. Its contents were astonishing:

> At Horebbeh which is in the Valley of Achor, under the steps, hidden eastwards, (at) forty cubits; a box of silver totalling 17 talents. (Column I, lines 1–4)
>
> In the tomb, in the third course of stones: 100 plates of gold. (I, 5–6)
>
> In the great cistern that is in the peristyle court, in its ground spout, is hidden in a box across from the upper entrance, 900 talents (I, 7–9).[8]

The scroll was indeed a list of buried treasure, sixty items in all, together with instructions on how to find them. But was it for real? Milik felt that the quantities listed were literally fantastic. For instance, in the first paragraph quoted above, "17 talents" of silver would be roughly half a ton. Could such an amount be simply put into a box and buried sixty feet ("forty cubits") deep? Perhaps, but Milik, de Vaux, and Cross developed a theory that the treasure of the *Copper Scroll* was a fiction, a folkloric indulgence of an ancient scribe describing an ideal treasure.[9]

Allegro thought their theory was as incredible as they thought the treasure to be, and could not believe it was seriously meant. He thought it was a cover-up to keep amateur treasure-hunters from combing through the Holy Land looking for the gold and silver. He also resented the fact that de Vaux had assigned the *Copper Scroll* to Milik for publication, and felt, perhaps justly, that this was due to the team's personal distrust of him.

Allegro believed de Vaux had to be removed from his dominant position. He outlined a plan in a letter to Awni Dajani,

Harding's successor, suggesting that the Department of Antiquities make a massive appeal for funds in order to buy more scrolls from the Bedouin, especially Cave 11 scrolls that they had not brought to the museum. The "new" scrolls would not be given to the Cave 4 team, but kept by Jordan. Together Allegro and Dajani would head a new team, and, if possible, proceed to take over the Palestine Museum itself. Allegro felt it "would be a ripe opportunity to take over the whole museum, scrolls and all." That would "break this Catholic monopoly" and mean "a lot of prestige coming your and the Department's way."[10]

Allegro also hoped to lure wealthy donors with the treasure of the *Copper Scroll*. He believed that he could identify the locations mentioned in the scroll and recover the treasure himself. Although the millionaire donors never materialized, he did receive some money from an English tabloid to underwrite an expedition, as well as Dajani's permission to excavate in Jordanian territory.

Allegro would not simply look for the ancient treasure, but also for additional scroll-bearing caves. New scrolls, besides confirming Allegro's merits as an archaeologist, would help him to realize yet another dream—building a new museum to house the Dead Sea Scrolls near the site of Khirbet Qumran itself.[11] A new facility might allow the Jordanian government to dissolve the international team, forming a new group with Allegro, not de Vaux, as head. This seems to have been Allegro's plan.

Unfortunately for Allegro, his expeditions in the winter of 1959–60 turned up nothing at all. He succeeded only in arousing the ire of de Vaux by spoiling part of the Khirbet Qumran excavation in his search for buried gold. He also caused a great deal of consternation in Jerusalem by proposing to dig on the Temple Mount, the ancient site of the Jewish temple, and since the seventh century A.D. the location of the Muslim mosque known as the Dome of the Rock. He was prevented from carrying out his plans by the intervention of Jordanian troops.[12]

Allegro's one success was publishing a transcription and translation of the *Copper Scroll* before Milik's officially sanctioned publication.[13] Although Milik had published translations of the scroll in French and English, Allegro's book *Treasure of the Copper Scroll* (1960) contained translations, transcriptions, drawings, and commentary. The credit (if that is the word) for the first "bootlegged" Dead Sea Scroll went to John Allegro.

De Vaux was furious at Allegro's end-run around his authority and had no admiration for either Allegro's translation of the *Copper Scroll* or his shoddy excavations.

> Mr. Allegro, speaking of the clandestine searches of the Bedouin, regrets that "a great deal of archaeological damage must already have been done in the course of this protracted amateur scroll hunting," (p. 131). But even more regrettable is the damage caused by his own "amateur treasure hunting." It is high time that this infantile behavior ceases and that we return to serious work.[14]

"As Rapidly as Can Be Expected"

"Serious work" is all very well, but "serious" seemed to mean "slow." Many expected the volumes that de Vaux had promised, *Discoveries from the Judean Desert,* to begin rolling off the presses long before the scrollery workroom was closed in 1960. In 1958, Millar Burrows wrote of his own expectations of a rapid publication. In the quote that follows, the actual publication date of the volumes mentioned is given in square brackets:

> The work of editing . . . [the] manuscript material from the region of the Dead Sea is now well advanced and proceeding as rapidly as can be expected in all the circumstances. The first volume, as we have noted, appeared in 1955. The second . . . may be published in 1958 [1962]. The third . . . , as well as the copper scroll, is not expected to appear before the end of 1959 [1962]. It is hoped that the remaining six or more volumes may be brought out at a rate of at least one a year.[15]

Burrows's estimate was wildly optimistic. By 1993, seven additional volumes of *DJD* had appeared, but the total number projected was twenty-six.

Since the team was too small and the work too demanding, the best solution would have been either to enlarge the team or lessen the work. There was no need to produce pages of commentary on each text. Once the fragments had been joined together and the text transcribed and translated, enough was available for a simple publication. But each member felt obliged to produce an "authoritative" interpretation of each and every piece of scroll.

De Vaux must bear some of the blame for the lack of direction. He was responsible for seeing that everyone did his assigned work, but apparently gave no deadlines. Indeed, he encouraged the team to slow down with their "preliminary" publications, lest the value and novelty of the forthcoming *DJD* volumes be diminished. De Vaux himself was preoccupied up to 1958 with excavating Khirbet Qumran and afterwards with other sites.

Another obstacle often mentioned, besides the team size, the workload, the uneven distribution of manuscripts, and Allegro's attempts to undercut the work of the others, was the question of funding. John D. Rockefeller, Jr., the founder of the Palestine Archaeological Museum, had contributed funds for the team's travel to and from Jerusalem and for their room and board while staying in Jerusalem to study the scrolls. When Rockefeller died in 1960, the grants ceased, and some members ceased coming to the museum for further work.

But was the end of Rockefeller support really an obstacle or just an excuse? Much of the work had been done by June 1960 anyway. The scrollery workroom was closed. Each team member had sets of photographs of the scrolls assigned to him. Although they are not as helpful as the real thing, good photographs of ancient texts are commonly used by scholars as the basis for their work. Some of the scrolls, in any case, could only be read in the photographs taken under infrared light. The team could have published their texts on the basis of the photographs. After all, most of the emerging research on the texts from Cave 1 were based on Trever's photographs.

Nevertheless, it is possible to exaggerate the "inactivity" of the team. Each member published at least one text, in preliminary form, in the early sixties. Allegro published several. Milik coauthored volumes 2 and 3 of *DJD*. But these publications were just a drop in the bucket. Scholars were clamoring for new Dead Sea Scrolls.

Although general public interest in the Dead Sea Scrolls had more or less played itself out by the sixties, the opposite was true among the international academic community. By 1957, over 3,000 scholarly articles and books had been written about the scrolls[16] and the following decade more than matched that number. A special journal, *Revue de Qumran,* was launched in 1958, solely devoted to the study of the Qumran literature. The study of the scrolls was a growth industry among scholars. The idea that a few colleagues were harboring hundreds of unpublished Dead Sea Scrolls, some of which might support (or worse, undermine) the research being done, was maddening. People began to complain.

De Vaux wrote a defense of the team's pace, pleading the volume and difficulty of the work. There were, after all, more than 15,000 fragments, the remains of more than 500 manuscripts. Although the team had succeeded in reconstructing and reading the texts,

> . . . the work of editing these incomplete and generally unique texts demands still a long period of study on the part of the team of scholars who joined the enterprise at the beginning but who also have other professional obligations. This work of editing is now in the process of completion and it is hoped that the publications will follow each other rapidly, while taking account of the capacity of each editor and of the exigencies of printing.[17]

De Vaux also told Edmund Wilson that he was going to put pressure on the team members to complete their assignments soon.[18]

Allegro also stepped up his attacks on the rest of the team. In August 1966, he published an article in *Harper's Magazine* called "The Untold Story of the Dead Sea Scrolls." In it he accused the Cave 4 team of withholding vital texts because they might have an adverse effect on Christianity:

> [T]he very scholars who should be most capable of working on the documents and interpreting them have displayed a not altogether surprising, but nonetheless curious, reluctance to go to the heart of the matter. The scholars appear to have held back from making discoveries which, there is evidence to believe, may upset a great many basic teachings of the Christian church.[19]

Allegro had no evidence that any of the Dead Sea Scrolls contained material damaging to Christianity, and his article provoked angry responses. Britain's top Old Testament scholars wrote a letter to the *Times* of London protesting Allegro's theories:

> Nothing that appears in the Scrolls hitherto discovered throws any doubt on the originality of Christianity. . . .The undersigned belong to different denominations or to none. They have no concern but to

> establish the truth and to see that these important documents are studied and evaluated with caution, scholarship, and a sense of proportion.[20]

Still, Allegro's gibes about the delay in publication hit home, and even those sympathetic to the team had to admit that it was high time the Cave 4 material was published. Joseph A. Fitzmyer, a Jesuit scholar and associate of the Cave 4 team, wrote of the "peculiar desire obsessing some of the members of the international team to say the last word on every text entrusted to them. . . . Instead of yielding to this desire, they should publish the texts with brief notes, and do so quickly."[21]

Allegro succeeded in one area. He persuaded the Jordanian government to nationalize the Palestine Archaeological Museum in 1966. Whether he could have further persuaded the Antiquities Department to sever its ties with de Vaux and the Ecole Biblique will never be known. War broke out in the Holy Land, and the museum and the scrolls fell into the hands of the Israelis.

The Six-Day War and After

The war began on June 5, 1967, and was over in less than a week. The Six-Day War was one of the shortest on record, but it completely changed the political situation in the Middle East. Israel gained control over the Sinai Peninsula, the Golan Heights, and the West Bank of Jordan. None of these acquisitions, however, meant as much to Jewish hearts as the unification of Jerusalem under Israeli auspices. For the first time since A.D. 70, the Holy City was entirely under Jewish control.

During the war, the Jordanians had fortified the Palestine Archaeological Museum and put gun emplacements in its main tower. The museum was strategically located outside the north-east corner of the Old City overlooking vital north-south roads in the Jerusalem area. On June 6, Israeli paratroopers entered the building and secured it after feeble Jordanian resistance. One lieutenant—like most Israelis keenly interested in archaeology—immediately began to search for the Dead Sea Scrolls, but the display case was empty.

Avraham Biran, director of the Israel Department of Antiquities, had received a call that same day from Carmella Yadin, Yigael

Yadin's wife. She told him that Yadin had been notified that the museum would soon be in Israeli hands and asked if Biran would go to the museum and make sure that the scrolls and other antiquities were safe.

Biran needed no arm-twisting. He took two other archaeologists with him to the museum, where they were obliged to go in the back door, since the paratroopers were still engaged in a fire-fight in the front with Jordanians on the city walls.

Some of the paratroopers immediately conscripted Biran to give them, during the battle, an impromptu lecture and tour of the antiquities of the museum. The archaeologist was happy to oblige and led a few of the soldiers around the premises, with the sound of shooting and breaking glass coming from the front of the building. The next day, after the entire city had been secured, the paratroopers left. Some of them dutifully signed the guest registry as they filed out, complete with banal comments ("Fantastic" "Very pleasant").[22]

Biran and the others could not find the scrolls. Weeks later, they were finally located in a basement safe behind a display case. The safe contained the Cave 4 and Cave 11 fragments. The *Copper Scroll* and some additional fragments from Cave 1 had been moved to the Amman Museum in Jordan, where they remain to this day.

The Cave 4 and Cave 11 scrolls were not the only ones to fall into Israeli hands. Visitors to Jerusalem in the weeks following the Six-Day War heard persistent rumors that Israeli troops had discovered more scrolls, perhaps an entire intact scroll. Nelson Glueck, at that time President of Hebrew Union College and an official of ASOR, heard a rumor in Kando's shop that a scroll of Genesis had been taken from the dealer. "I am gathering information about this mystery story," wrote Glueck in his journal, "and it promises to be a whiz-bang account."[23]

When the whole story finally came out, it proved to be indeed a "whiz-bang account."[24] Cave 11, like Cave 1, had yielded some virtually intact scrolls; but when the cave was discovered, the authorities had trouble raising funds to buy them from the Bedouin. Rumors persisted that some complete scrolls were never offered to the museum for sale.

The rumors were partially true. Kando had withheld one sizable scroll—the largest of all the Dead Sea Scrolls. Kando also retained pieces he had torn from the other Cave 11 scrolls.[25] It appears that he hoped to sell the large scroll to a private collector and make a large fortune, as he had already made a small one from selling Cave 4 pieces.

Kando chose for a go-between an American televangelist named Joe Uhrig, whom he had met on one of Uhrig's trips to the Holy Land. Uhrig was popular in the U.S. and counted a number of celebrities among his friends and viewers. Kando evidently believed Uhrig could find a millionaire buyer for his scroll. Uhrig, however, wanted the scroll to go to Israel. In August 1960 he wrote to an astonished Yigael Yadin, offering to open negotiations on behalf of Kando for unknown Dead Sea Scrolls. The asking price for the large scroll was one million dollars. Yadin, of course, required some convincing of the validity of the offer. Uhrig sent Yadin a photo of a piece of scroll (it later turned out to be from the Cave 11 Psalms Scroll). Finally convinced that Kando had a real scroll to offer, Yadin began trying to bargain down the price.

By November 1961 Yadin and Uhrig had come to agree on a price of $130,000. Uhrig went to Jordan to complete the transaction with Kando, but to Uhrig's and Yadin's dismay, the antiquities dealer backed out and demanded yet more money. Although Uhrig continued to try to get Kando to honor the original terms of the deal, by May 1962 the transaction was dead.

Years went by, and Yadin had just about given up all hope of ever seeing the scroll he had made a $10,000 deposit on. But in the wake of Israel's takeover of the West Bank, he realized that Kando's shops in East Jerusalem and Bethlehem now lay within Israeli jurisdiction. He sent soldiers to investigate. On Kando's property they found a shoe box containing the large scroll. It had begun to deteriorate badly from exposure to dampness. A cigar box held further fragments, and more pieces of the scroll were later found hidden behind the frames of family photographs. The scroll was handed over to Yadin, who took possession of it on behalf of the government of Israel.

Ten years later Yadin finally published the text of what he called the *Temple Scroll*, a composition based on the legal portions of the Pentateuch, along with detailed instructions for the building of God's ideal temple in Jerusalem. The *Temple Scroll* is the longest of all the Dead Sea Scrolls (sixty-six columns), and scholars are still divided over its significance. Some believe that the Jewish sect that produced the scroll considered it to be Scripture on a par with the other books of the Old Testament. Others assign it a lesser place, attributing it to a different group than the one that produced the *Manual of Discipline* and other well-known writings from Qumran. It is, in any case, a text of surpassing interest to scholars.

The *Temple Scroll,* however, and the rest of the Dead Sea Scrolls, continued to be a bone of contention between Jordan and Israel for years afterwards. On the Israeli side, there was a general spirit of self-congratulation on acquiring not only the Dead Sea Scrolls, but the Palestine Archaeological Museum as well. The grandest prizes of all, from the archaeological point of view, were East Jerusalem and the West Bank, containing some of the choicest historical sites connected with the Bible. Now these were accessible to Israeli archaeologists. The Jordanians, for their part, considered all Israeli plans to dig in the West Bank as so many Zionist plots to deface Jordanian antiquities; and the theft, as they saw it, of the *Temple Scroll* was particularly galling.[26] At the October 1969 meeting of the United Nations Educational, Scientific, and Cultural Organization (UNESCO) the Jordanian delegate made an official claim to the scroll on behalf of the Kingdom of Jordan.

The Israelis considered Jordan's claim to the *Temple Scroll* and the rest of the Dead Sea Scrolls laughable. One Israeli archaeologist wrote triumphantly, "Israel now has both Jerusalem and the Museum, and can proudly say that all of the priceless Dead Sea Scrolls, written in the national language of Israel, are in the best possible hands."[27] Yadin said that "the Scrolls . . . could hardly be regarded as an intrinsic part of Jordanian culture, heritage, or possession."[28]

In any case, the change of government was a *fait accompli*. The name of the Palestine Archaeological Museum was changed to the Rockefeller Museum, which was what everyone always called it anyway. The Jerusalem branch of ASOR also changed its name to the W. F. Albright Institute to give at least an impression of independence from the ASOR branches in Arab countries.

Many archaeologists and scholars found the changes hard to accept. Among them were the pro-Arab Roland de Vaux and several members of the Cave 4 team, particularly Skehan, Starcky, and Milik. (John Allegro was also fiercely anti-Israel, but by 1968 all of his Cave 4 material was already in print.) De Vaux at first refused to carry on with his work at the Ecole Biblique in protest of the Israeli occupation. Patrick Skehan, whose biblical texts were ready to go to the printer for his *DJD* volume, refused to publish them under Israeli auspices. The work of the international team temporarily ground to a halt, although Yadin and Biran had promised not to interfere with their work. Many other pro-Arab archaeologists also refused to work in Israel.

Others adapted themselves to the new situation. ASOR continued to sponsor excavations under the Israel Department of Antiquities. Eventually, de Vaux began to come around and, in 1971, embarked on a major dig at Tel Kisan north of Haifa. But that same year his health began to fail, and in September he died of a coronary thrombosis. W. F. Albright had passed away less than two weeks earlier.

Notes

1. Geza Vermes, *The Dead Sea Scrolls: Qumran in Perspective* (Philadelphia: Fortress, 1977), 24.

2. Jordan also announced at this time that the scrolls would not be allowed to leave the country. The government promised institutions that had donated money to the Department of Antiquities and to the museum that they would get their money back. It is not clear whether all were in fact repaid. Canada's McGill University, for example, which had raised $20,000 to purchase 436 pieces from 160 different manuscripts, was reimbursed only after the Vatican and Roland de Vaux intervened on its behalf (Eileen Schuller, "The 40th Anniversary of the Dead Sea Scrolls," *Studies in Religion/Sciences Religeuses* 18 [1989]: 63).

3. The figures are drawn from the list compiled by Stephen A. Reed and Marilyn Lundberg of the Ancient Biblical Manuscript Center of Claremont, California, 1991.

4. John Allegro, *Treasure of the Copper Scroll,* rev. ed. (New York: Doubleday, 1964), 32.

5. Cross, *Ancient Library of Qumran,* 45–46.

6. *The Dead Sea Scrolls After Forty Years,* Symposium at the Smithsonian Institution, 27 October 1990 (Washington, D.C.: Biblical Archaeology Society, 1991), 78.

7. Skehan, "Capriccio Allegro, or How Not to Learn in Ten Years," *Christian Century* 83 (5 October 1966): 1211.

8. The translations are given according to the text given by B. Z. Lurie, *Megillat ha-Nehoshet* (The Copper Scroll) (Jerusalem: Kiryath Sepher, 1963).

9. Cross, *Ancient Library of Qumran,* 20–25.

10. Letter from Allegro to Awni Dajani, 10 January 1959.

11. *Jerusalem Post,* 13 April 1961, 3.

12. Wilson, *Israel and the Dead Sea Scrolls,* 283. Allegro apparently believed that de Vaux, of all people, was responsible for calling out the Jordanian troops (see the revised edition of his *Treasure of the Copper Scroll,* 131), which illustrates his paranoia in any area where de Vaux was concerned.

13. According to Michael Baigent and Richard Leigh, *The Dead Sea Scrolls Deception* (London: Jonathan Cape, 1991), the first translation of the *Copper Scroll* was published by Allegro himself (p. 55). In fact, the first translation was published by Milik in the journal *Revue Biblique* in 1959. Baigent and Leigh make no mention at all of Allegro's plan to find the treasure himself, or of his utter failure to do so. In fact, all of Allegro's archeological misadventures are passed over in silence in *The Dead Sea Scrolls Deception.*

14. R. de Vaux, review of Allegro, *Treasure of the Copper Scroll,* in *Revue Biblique* 68 (1961): 147.

15. Millar Burrows, *More Light on the Dead Sea Scrolls* (New York: Viking, 1958), 34.

16. For a listing, see William Sanford LaSor's *Bibliography of the Dead Sea Scrolls 1948–1957,* Fuller Theological Seminary Bibliographical Series No. 2 (Fall 1958).

17. Quoted by P. Benoit in the preface to *Discoveries in the Judean Desert VI* (Oxford: Oxford University Press, 1977), v.

18. Wilson, *Israel and the Dead Sea Scrolls,* 262.

19. John Allegro, "The Untold Story of the Dead Sea Scrolls," *Harper's Magazine* (August 1966): 46.

20. "The Dead Sea Scrolls: Significance for Scholars," *Times* of London, 21 December 1965. The signers were G. R. Driver (who had recommended Strugnell for the team), H. H. Rowley (who had recommended Allegro), Peter Ackroyd, Matthew Black, J. B. Segal, D. Winton Thomas, and Edward Ullendorff. The nonsectarian makeup of this group is shown by the presence of Jewish scholars Segal and Ullendorff.

21. J. A. Fitzmyer, "A Sample of Scrollduggery," *America* (3 September 1966): 228. Skehan's critique of Allegro was the one entitled "Capriccio Allegro" cited above. It demonstrates one of the amusing sidelights of this phase of the controversy: the irresistible desire felt by some to make puns on Allegro's name. It is said that one of Allegro's colleagues, referring to his well-known penchant for jumping to conclusions, admonished him: "Allegro, *adagio, adagio!*"

22. The details about the seizing of the museum and Biran's visit there have been taken from J. Robert Moskin, *Among Lions: The Battle for Jerusalem, June 5–7, 1967* (New York: Arbor House, 1982), and Abraham Rabinovich, *The Battle for Jerusalem, June 5–7, 1967,* rev. ed. (Philadelphia: Jewish Publication Society, 1987).

23. Nelson Glueck, *Dateline: Jerusalem* (Cincinnati: Hebrew Union College Press, 1968), 56–57.

24. Most of the details in the following narrative are found in Yigael Yadin, *The Temple Scroll: The Hidden Law of the Dead Sea Sect* (New York: Random House, 1985); and Hershel Shanks, "Intrigue and the Scroll: Behind the Scenes of Israel's Acquisition of the Temple Scroll," *Biblical Archaeology Review* (November/December 1987): 23–27.

25. Some of these pieces were still emerging as recently as 1992, when Bruce Zuckerman of the University of Southern California revealed the discovery of a lost fragment of the Cave 11 *Targum of Job.*

26. There were accusations that Kando was imprisoned for a short time to induce him to give information about where other Dead Sea Scrolls might be hidden. Glueck's account, based on his conversations with Kando immediately after the Six-Day War, seems reliable. He states that Kando was taken to Tel Aviv and confined in a "nice apartment" for five days while the authorities interrogated him. The Israelis finally became convinced that Kando had no more scrolls in his possession and released him (*Dateline: Jerusalem,* 118–19). Glueck advised Kando to get a lawyer and sue for the price of the scroll. Kando did so, and eventually the government of Israel paid the dealer $105,000.

27. Dov Peretz Elkins, "Archaeology After the Six-Day War," *American Zionist* (November 1968): 23.

28. Yigael Yadin, letter in the *Times* of London, 27 August 1969: quoted by Paul Lapp, "Captive Treasures," *Mid East* (February 1970): 41.

Chapter 4

The Rediscovery of the Dead Sea Scrolls

The leadership of the Cave 4 team fell to Pierre Benoit, another French Catholic scholar from the Ecole Biblique. Benoit was determined to see the team's work carried through to completion. He began negotiations with Yadin and Biran to allow publication of the scrolls under conditions that satisfied the objections of the pro-Arab team members. The Israelis insisted that the name of the publication—till then, *Discoveries in the Judean Desert of Jordan*—drop all mention of Jordan in the title. In return the official publication would make no mention of Israel at all, beyond acknowledging the new cosponsorship of the Shrine of the Book, Israel's Dead Sea Scrolls museum. An official agreement to resume publication of the *DJD* series was finally achieved in January 1973. One scholar, hailing the new accord, predicted that "now, with a little luck and patience, the authoritative scrolls will finally be publicly available."[1]

Only five volumes of *DJD* had been published by 1973. Only one volume, containing Allegro's lot of manuscripts, included any Cave 4 material. While the *DJD* series was in limbo between 1967 and 1973, Milik prepared his manuscripts of the *Book of Enoch* as a separate publication, appearing in 1976. Although containing much of Milik's customary brilliance, the volume was in general a bloated mess, encumbered by long historical and literary discussions that many reviewers felt added nothing to the interpretation of the fragments. Although specialists were excited by the Aramaic texts, many felt that Milik's book was an example of the kind of scholarly overkill that the Cave 4 team evidently had in mind for all the scrolls.

With Benoit's prodding, volume six of *DJD* was published in 1977. To the disappointment of many, it contained only some archaeological observations on Cave 4 left behind by de Vaux, and the texts of *tefillin* and *mezuzot* from Cave 4. *Tefillin,* or phylacteries, are the small boxes worn by Jews on the forehead and arm during times of prayer, and contain verses from Exodus and Deuteronomy. *Mezuzot* are similar boxes affixed to doorways. Though interested in these texts, the scholarly world had not been waiting for them with bated breath, especially when one insider had promised that *all* of Milik's Cave 4 texts were already at the publishers.[2]

Perhaps because of the general disappointment with these unkept promises, the seventies saw an increase in the public and academic complaints about the rate of publication of the Cave 4 texts. The thirtieth anniversary of the discovery of the first cave provided the occasion for Prof. Geza Vermes's remarks quoted in part at the beginning of the previous chapter:

> On this thirtieth anniversary of their first coming to light the world is entitled to ask the authorities responsible for the publication of the Qumran Scrolls and the Bar Kokhba documents[3] what they intend to do about this lamentable state of affairs. For unless drastic measures are taken at once, the greatest and most valuable of all Hebrew and Aramaic manuscript discoveries is likely to become the academic scandal *par excellence* of the twentieth century.[4]

This quotation rapidly became as widely quoted as Albright's dictum about "the greatest manuscript discovery of modern times." Together these remarks sum up the story of Dead Sea Scrolls research, at least as it is popularly perceived.

Adding his voice to the growing outcry was David Noel Freedman, a former student of Albright's and a friend and colleague of Frank Cross. ASOR had given him the responsibility to publish one of the Cave 11 scrolls. Hence he was to some extent an "insider." His editorial in the September 1977 issue of the *Biblical*

Archaeologist[5] was therefore a significant index of the frustration many felt. Freedman took note of the long wait for the Cave 4 material, questioning whether "a single scholar, or a small group can or should have the exclusive right to study and publish inscriptional materials at their own pleasure and discretion. . . . [S]uch a monopolistic system . . . has not proved successful." He went on to call for the prompt publication, without commentary, of all new finds "within one year of discovery," confessing:

> I write as a guilty party, since I was assigned responsibility for the Leviticus Scroll from Cave 11 about ten years ago. There have been some diplomatic and other complications, but basically, the reason this document has not been published is that I was overloaded with other obligations and commitments which claimed my time. That is not an excuse, and I should either have published the scroll or returned it to the team for reassignment. Many if not most scholars harbor optimistic delusions about what they can and will do in the way of productive writing, and even after observing many colleagues fall into the pit, I have followed the same primrose path.[6]

Freedman's remarks were a telling indictment of the status quo. By 1977 it had been more than twenty years since Cross, for instance, had published any texts from his allotment. Starcky and Strugnell had published almost nothing of their assignments. Skehan published a text in 1977, his first in almost two decades.[7]

By contrast, Allegro, for all his mischief, had completed the publication of his texts by 1968. Milik continued steadily to publish pieces from his group of texts, as well as his *Books of Enoch* volume. Outside the official team, Yadin published the *Temple Scroll*. Many of the other texts from Cave 11 had been published by 1977, including the scroll of Psalms and the Targum (Aramaic translation) of Job. So although the Cave 4 team deserved much of the criticism that came its way, the talk of "scandal" was an exaggeration. Scholars did not lack for new material to work on.

Under Benoit, the team expanded to include collaborators, sometimes against Benoit's better judgment.

> I [Strugnell] had started in 1979 pushing to get some of my larger groups [of manuscripts] passed to my doctoral students. My principle there was that I made the decision who should have this material and then I notified Benoit. Benoit himself didn't encourage the process.

> He was a little hesitant about getting these younger scholars, instead of people of riper judgment. But he didn't make any objection.[8]

The first Israeli collaborators, Emanuel Tov and Elisha Qimron, were brought on board during Benoit's tenure.

However, once the word *scandal* had been used, it continued to be used. There were even suggestions that the principally Catholic complexion of the team had something to do with the slow pace of publication. Were there certain texts among the unpublished scrolls that were damaging to the faith? Could religious scholars—especially priests—be trusted with explosive documents of this sort?

Most of these allegations can be traced back to Allegro. He had always hinted that his religious colleagues were capable of suppressing "dangerous" discoveries. (Of course, when his "dangerous" texts were published, they contained nothing like the implications he read into them.) The real reason for the delay was the mundane, even banal, explanation Freedman admitted to: They just couldn't get around to it.

Nevertheless, Allegro's accusations kept coming, and others began to join him, especially when the eighties began and no new texts were being released. Benoit, stung by the accusations of Allegro and others, responded angrily:

> Nothing will be hidden, and there is nothing to hide. It would be perverse to make the public believe that there exists in our care some mysterious documents whose publication would be fatal to religion. Nothing of the sort exists.[9]

Benoit admitted that the team had been working more slowly than he wished, but that he expected complete manuscripts soon from Milik and Eugene Ulrich, a former student of Cross's who filled Skehan's position on the team after he died in 1980. He noted that Strugnell (who had become a colleague of Cross at Harvard in 1980) came to Jerusalem yearly to work on his manuscripts, and he expressed the hope—rather frigidly, one feels—that Cross and Starcky would succeed in freeing themselves from other obligations in order to work on their assignments.

Benoit's protest came out on the heels of another *DJD* volume, this one by Maurice Baillet, who therewith completed his assigned Cave 4 texts. Although the publication of Baillet's texts seemed to bode well for Benoit's promised speedup of publication,

Vermes (the "academic scandal" man) fumed over the wasted time (and high price) it took to publish a book of what he believed to be mainly "meaningless bits and pieces . . . useless scraps."[10] Benoit, in any case, had done well not to promise a miracle, since, as the eighties went on, no additional Dead Sea Scrolls were published.

In 1986, Avraham Eitan, the successor to Avraham Biran as director of Israel's Antiquities Department, met with Benoit and asked for a detailed progress report. The Israelis had promised de Vaux in 1967 that they would not interfere with the work of the team, but de Vaux was gone, and the team had not done its work. The long delay had begun to reflect badly on Israeli management of the situation, and it is easy to see that Eitan's request reflects a growing restlessness within the archaeological establishment in Israel. Although Eitan got his progress report from Benoit, we do not know what impact it might have had. Eitan left the directorship, and Benoit died in 1987. Benoit was succeeded by his deputy John Strugnell, who had already been *de facto* director of the team—with Benoit's and the team's consent—for the last few years.

John Strugnell: "Enough Work to Do"

If the thirtieth anniversary had provoked Vermes's "academic scandal" accusation, the fortieth saw the anger of biblical scholars reach the boiling point. Vermes sponsored a conference on the Dead Sea Scrolls in London. With Cross, Strugnell, and Ulrich in the audience, he called for the immediate publication of all photographs of the scrolls, without commentary, transcription, or editorial material, so that

> the charge of weakness or procrastination on the part of the editor-in-chief would be lifted from his shoulders, and the other editors also would escape being accused of displaying a kind of proprietary attitude towards an immense cultural treasure whose trustees they are, but which in fact belongs to us all.[11]

Strugnell, the new editor-in-chief, rejected any suggestion of procrastination, and in most of his comments in the months and years following, showed himself a pugnacious defender of the rights, privileges, and performance of the team he had been a part of since the beginning.

> Instead of complaining about our slowness, I would suggest that scholars devote themselves to a careful reading of the books that have already been published. . . . I therefore close this report with the suggestion that there is enough work to do—not only for me but also for you.[12]

But regardless of Strugnell's feelings, the Israelis began exercising more active supervision of the project than ever before. Succeeding Eitan as Antiquities Director was General Amir Drori, a former Deputy Chief of Staff, and the Department of Antiquities was changed to the more powerful Israel Antiquities Authority (IAA). Drori appointed a three-man scrolls advisory committee of Israeli scholars to keep tabs on the work of the Cave 4 team and to insure that the work was kept on schedule.

Under Strugnell, the team was adding more collaborators. Cross had asked Ulrich for his help in preparing his lot for publication, and Ulrich consented with the proviso that they would train qualified graduate students to help with the enormous task.[13] In Ulrich's view, the students made ideal assistants because they had no other academic obligations to hamper their concentration as well as compelling professional reasons to finish quickly. Strugnell too farmed out some texts to his students, and collaborated with Israeli scholars on the texts entrusted to him.

Nevertheless, the critics of the Cave 4 team continued to grow in number and vehemence. As the pace of publishing "preliminary editions" picked up, the focus of the attack broadened from the issue of delay to access. Many scholars resented the fact that graduate students, traditionally at the bottom of the academic pecking order, were being given access to the Dead Sea Scrolls, while senior "outsider" scholars were not. Part of this was sheer envy. The original Cave 4 team had all been young when they started—Allegro, Strugnell, and Milik had been, in effect, graduate students—and no one had complained then.

There were less ignoble motives, of course. The first generation of Dead Sea Scrolls scholars had begun to give way to a second generation. De Vaux and Albright had died in 1971; Burrows and Skehan in 1980; Yadin and Brownlee in 1984; Benoit in 1987; Starcky and Allegro in 1988. Skehan's texts had been "inherited" by Eugene Ulrich (Cross's former student), Starcky's by Emile Puech, also of the Ecole Biblique. The old guard was disappearing, but the old order was not. It looked like it was being passed on to a new group of privileged insiders. This was aggravating, both to the aging "outsiders" who still had not seen texts discovered when they were young, and to the up-and-coming young outsiders who were left out.

The criticism was also in part rooted in the fear among outsiders that their books and articles about the Dead Sea Scrolls might be weakened or proved wrong when the Cave 4 texts finally were made public. They wanted access to the scrolls or photos to verify their own work. Their concern was heightened when Strugnell and collaborator Elisha Qimron made public in 1985 information about an unpublished scroll, known as 4QMMT,[14] having important implications for the history and law of the Qumran sect.

But sheer intellectual curiosity was the main reason behind the criticism. The prospect of new and fascinating information about a crucial period in world and religious history continued to animate most critics. And, of course, no one *likes* being an outsider.

The team members were not opposed in principle to allowing access to the scrolls to those they thought qualified. Over the years, Cross provided information on the biblical texts to most scholars who asked for it. Even the pro-Arab Skehan had made available to the Hebrew University Bible Project all his transcriptions of the Cave 4 Isaiah texts as early as 1955.

> It depended on the practice of the individual editors. At this point we passed texts on to people we thought could use the material. It was a judgment of quality. The Hebrew University team was obviously very serious. If someone from the Bible Belt wanted to know about the Virgin Birth in Isaiah, we didn't take so much speed in answering that piece of mail. Certainly there was an element of elitism in this.[15]

But the team eventually feared that even limited access to the scrolls would open the floodgates to mass bootlegging of texts. In the early eighties, Martin Abegg, then a student at the Hebrew University, was allowed to study some unpublished biblical scrolls, but was cautioned: "Don't show these to anybody else!" As critics multiplied, the team tended to close ranks to preserve its own privileges. Strugnell in particular became increasingly disdainful of outsider attacks.

One of the most vociferous critics of the team was Hershel Shanks, publisher of the *Biblical Archaeology Review* (*BAR*). *BAR* began publication in 1978 and quickly won admirers for its combination of beautiful photographs and popular articles on archaeology and the Bible. Shanks's ambition to have up-to-the-minute reports on archaeological discoveries sometimes brought him into conflict with professionals more used to the leisurely academic pace. He did not hesitate to denounce those he thought were impeding the public's right to know quickly. Though Shanks had sporadically noted the publication delays in *BAR* in the past, by 1989 he had decided to make the sins of the Cave 4 team a regular topic of complaint.

Another sharp critic of the Cave 4 team was Robert Eisenman of California State University in Long Beach. Eisenman, a historian who interested himself in scrolls research, attacked the "insiders" along some of the same lines as had Allegro: that Dead Sea Scrolls research was being shaped by Roman Catholic biases and was suffering as a result. Like Allegro, Eisenman's own approach to the interpretation of the scrolls was widely considered to be idiosyncratic. And, like Allegro, the agnostic Eisenman also hoped to pry the texts loose from the official team. But unlike Allegro, Eisenman was to see his ambition realized.

In March 1989, Eisenman wrote to Strugnell requesting access to some of the Cave 4 manuscripts of the *Damascus Document,* claiming that "it is an imposition upon us and a hardship to ask us to wait any longer for . . . these materials." When Strugnell turned him down, Eisenman complained to Gen. Drori and wrote another angry letter to Strugnell, who replied disdainfully:

> I don't propose spending time in correcting the factual errors and understandings you make about the history of the Qumran Editorial Project; I have rarely seen more per page—they do not improve your reputation for competence in these matters. . . . As a rule I do not write answers to public letters—I make just this one exception in your case, hoping that it will inspire you in any further letters to follow politer and more acceptable norms.[16]

In fact, Eisenman had no intent or expectation of receiving scrolls from Strugnell. His main purpose was to have a documented refusal as a basis for filing a lawsuit against the team in the Israeli courts, a plan he later dropped. "We wanted to be turned down; we expected to be turned down."[17]

Eisenman showed his correspondence to Shanks, who eagerly publicized it in *BAR*. Shanks's articles in his widely distributed magazine served as a megaphone for Eisenman's complaints, and the world press began to show interest in this scholarly catfight. In the United States, the *New York Times, Washington Post,* and *Time* ran articles on the controversy. The Dead Sea Scrolls, so long absent from the public eye, began to creep back into the spotlight.

Scrollduggery

Ironically, if anyone but Eisenman had requested access to the scrolls, Strugnell might well have considered it. He thought Eisenman unqualified to interpret the Qumran texts; and in fact Eisenman admittedly does not have the linguistic and paleographic training necessary to read the Dead Sea manuscripts. Furthermore, many people suspected that Eisenman had leaked to the scholarly public a transcription of 4QMMT, as well as a private printout of Cave 4 documents.[18] So when Eisenman promised Strugnell not to publish any photographs he was given, Strugnell, from his standpoint, had every reason to be wary.[19]

In any case, the anti-team sentiments built up by the Shanks-Eisenman attacks continued to make themselves felt in scholarly circles throughout 1989. A colloquium on the Dead Sea Scrolls held in Mogilany, Poland, in September issued a statement (the "Mogilany Resolution") deploring the ongoing delay in publication and proposing that those responsible "publish the plates of all as yet unpublished material . . . in advance of the accompanying definitive critical editions."[20] Shanks gave the resolution a prominent place in *BAR*.

Shanks showed himself to be a hard man to please. Though he had called for a release of the original publication timetable (*BAR*, May/June 1989), when it was released, he denounced it as a "hoax and a fraud" (July/August 1989). He repeatedly called for reassignment of the texts to more scholars, then, when it was done, criticized the process as being made on the "buddy-boy" system (September/October 1989). He identified Milik and Strugnell as the main "bottleneck" in the process (September/October 1989), but when Milik reassigned some of his texts to two American scholars, Shanks pilloried the two in *BAR* for not making their texts accessible enough to others. When the young scholar Stephen Reed began to make a long-overdue catalog of all the Cave 4 texts, Shanks both hailed the move and complained that *BAR* was not notified fast enough.

Because of his magazine's high circulation and its racy, popular style, Shanks was able to influence most of the public conversation about the scrolls for months. A *New York Times* editorial dealing with the issue ("The Vanity of Scholars," 9 July 1989) was simply a paraphrase of past *BAR* editorials. There and elsewhere the team was depicted as a bunch of haughty snobs, greedily hoarding priceless manuscripts while thumbing their noses at the general public—a picture that had an element of truth, but overlooked several positive steps taken since Benoit's death.

But Shanks at this time knew something very few other people knew: Eisenman possessed hundreds of secretly obtained photographs of the Dead Sea Scrolls.

A person or persons in Jerusalem with access to a set of photographs—Eisenman will not reveal the names[21]—sympathized with Eisenman's crusade to gain access to the scrolls. The photos started coming to Eisenman through the mail in October 1989, as he says, "slowly, in little packets at first, and then more extensively." Eisenman now had no need to pursue a lawsuit in the Israeli courts. He revealed his secret to only a few people, including Shanks. The editor of *BAR* kept Eisenman's secret for months while continuing to write editorials castigating the official team for keeping theirs.

Eisenman also had to take someone else into his confidence—someone who actually had the training to read the photos he possessed. In November 1990, he mentioned his growing cache of photos to a young scholar, Michael O. Wise of the University of Chicago. Wise, a specialist in the Dead Sea Scrolls, agreed to give Eisenman the benefit of his expertise in exchange for access to Eisenman's photos.

While spending a week at Eisenman's home in Long Beach in December 1990, Wise was astonished to discover that "he had everything—over 1,700 photographs! They were stacked up on his desk, sitting on bookcases, everywhere."[22] Wise, who thought he would never be allowed to read these texts, set about the work of transcribing and translating. The "charmed circle" of scroll insiders had been broken, but hardly anyone was yet aware of it.

Meanwhile, back in Jerusalem, the Israeli authorities had been having trouble with John Strugnell. (Strugnell had a poster on the wall of his room at the Ecole Biblique: a picture of a rhinoceros with the caption "I may have my faults, but being wrong isn't one of them.") Although he had actively pushed the team to pick up the pace and to reassign texts, he didn't like taking orders from the IAA, which was increasingly inclined to give them.

Actually, the IAA and Strugnell wanted the same thing: more reassignments and collaborators leading to a more rapid publication of the scrolls, but they differed on management styles. The IAA wanted to bureaucratize the process, with fixed timelines, chains of command, and ultimate accountability to the IAA. Strugnell favored a more informal procedure, where each editor decided the fate of his own allotment.

But Strugnell also saw the Cave 4 team as an international endeavor. He felt the Israelis, like the Jordanians, were trying to take over the project for national ends. For Strugnell, an Israeli takeover of the Cave 4 team was not much different, in principle, from Yadin's raid on Kando's shop. Only the names of the generals had changed.

Strugnell's occasional public statements on the scrolls yielded mostly bad publicity for the team; for instance, in an interview with ABC News, he contemptuously dismissed the outsiders as "a bunch of fleas who are in the business of annoying us." Shanks gleefully pounced on this statement and put Strugnell's picture, surrounded by fleas, on the cover of *BAR* (March/April 1990).[23]

The authorities began to look at Strugnell—who reportedly then suffered from alcoholism and manic-depressive episodes—as an obstruction. A showdown of some sort seemed inevitable in the fall of 1990 when the IAA, over Strugnell's objections and without conferring with the other editors, prepared to appoint an Israeli scholar, Emanuel Tov, as the coeditor-in-chief of the international team.

But before this power play could unfold, in October Strugnell gave an interview to a reporter from the Israeli newspaper *Ha-Aretz*. In it he not only criticized the state of Israel, but also denounced Judaism as a religion:

> Q: What bothers you about Judaism?
>
> A: Judaism. That's all. The fact that it survives. It should have disappeared. Christianity now uses much more irenic language for all this. These are brutal terms; I'm putting it in harsh terms. For me the solution to the Jewish problem is mass conversion. . . .
>
> Q: But what in Judaism bothers you so much?
>
> A: Why, nothing. I'm Catholic, and the fact that you don't eat pork just leaves more for me. . . . What bothers me is the subsistence of the group, of Jews, of the Jewish religion. It's a horrible religion. It's a Christian heresy, and we deal with our heretics in different ways.

The interview was published in Israel on November 9, 1990, and an English version was published in the January/February 1991 issue of *BAR*.[24] Strugnell's words sent a shock wave of repugnance through the scholarly community. His friends, both Jews and Christians, could not believe these statements were sincerely meant or uttered when his mind was clear; but clearly Strugnell had to go. The IAA removed him from his post on December 30, and Emanuel Tov became the fourth editor-in-chief of the Cave 4 team.

"Things I Want to See"

Meanwhile, Jewish scholar Ben Zion Wacholder of Hebrew Union College in Cincinnati, Ohio, and graduate student Martin Abegg had begun their own efforts to gain access to the scrolls. In 1989 the two scholars were working on a second fragmentary copy of the *Temple Scroll* from Cave 11. They had gotten unexpected permission from the Royal Dutch Academy, owners of the publication rights, to publish this unreleased text. The Rockefeller Museum staff was so cooperative in providing photographs that Wacholder and Abegg began to feel that a new wind was beginning to blow from Jerusalem. In early 1991 they optimistically ordered photos of all the unpublished texts from Cave 11. But after Strugnell's ouster, a new mentality was in evidence in the IAA. Their request was turned down.

Disappointed, Wacholder and Abegg turned to another source of information about the unpublished texts: a private concordance of the texts from Caves 2–10. At Strugnell's urging, the official team had brought in several young scholars in the late fifties to make a concordance of all the unpublished texts that had been reconstructed and transcribed to that point. Years later, when Strugnell had become chief editor, he allowed copies of the concordance to be made and distributed to institutions where the scrolls were studied.[25] One of them was Hebrew Union College. As Abegg tells it,

> The concordance was put in the stacks in October of 1990. . . . I was hoping that it wasn't just a word-list, without sentence contexts. I thought, "It's going to be nice, but it's not going to be that helpful." But when I saw it, my first thought was, "I can reconstruct things I want to see."[26]

About the time Michael Wise was reading Eisenman's photos, Abegg began to reconstruct the texts of particular scrolls he was interested in. Using an off-the-shelf database program on his home computer, he was able to input the word-lists with their surrounding contexts and then use the computer to reconstitute the original transcription.

> As I was reconstructing the material I reported fairly frequently to Dr. Wacholder what I was doing. He didn't send me to do it. I did it on my own, basically, and he really wasn't all that excited about it at first, until we had whole texts. And then he realized, "This is good stuff, it's very usable material." From that time started the process: What do we do with it?

The thrill of seeing material that had long been held privately was soon followed by a sense of the injustice that had been committed against the outsider scholars.

> From my own perspective, working with Dr. Wacholder, I was struck by the travesty of it, and realizing that this fellow could have used the material for the last 30 years and it had been kept from him. That was very important to me, that there were other people like that. . . . So of course Wacholder immediately said, "Let's publish it." But I really hung back at first.

In the spring of 1991, Abegg began to confer with his friends, colleagues, and members of his church about what to do. Some—including this author—advised him, for the sake of his career, not to publish. Others were more favorable.

> In the back of our minds all this time, we knew that if we called up Hershel Shanks, that he would be up that afternoon! Finally, we sent the manuscript to Hershel, who agreed to publish it.

> My initial feeling was that I wanted to input the whole concordance before we published anything, because I was sure I would miss things if I were just searching for particular texts. But Shanks was pushing to publish it as fast as possible. And his word at the time was, "There are other people doing this sort of thing. It's all going to break open pretty soon."

Shanks was referring to the work of Eisenman and James Robinson, another scholar in California, who agreed to help Eisenman edit his collection of under-the-table photos for publication. While Abegg was agonizing over whether to publish or not, Eisenman and Robinson had made their own arrangements with E. J. Brill, a scholarly press in Holland, to publish the photos in April.

But at a conference on the scrolls in Madrid in March, a controversy erupted over a bootleg text of 4QMMT published by the Polish journal, *The Qumran Chronicle*. The team threatened its editor with legal action and forced him to withdraw the bootleg text. This event evidently caused consternation in the Brill offices, and caused them to cancel the Eisenman-Robinson project two weeks before the publication date.

> Robinson and I were distraught, we were just shattered. We were so close. At this point, we didn't know anything about the Wacholder-Abegg project. Shanks whispered something about it to me. . . . But we were going to beat them, too. We were going to make it all available—not just a reconstruction, but all the pictures.[27]

Frustrated, Eisenman and Robinson turned to Hershel Shanks to publish their project, as had Wacholder and Abegg. Shanks was eager to comply. Though Eisenman was anxious to get his photos out before anyone else, he had to put publication on hold again to raise the several thousand dollars Shanks required to defray the publishing costs.

So as the summer of 1991 wore on, the Dead Sea Scrolls were on the brink of publication. Abegg patiently typed in the entire concordance in Cincinnati while Eisenman sought backers in California.

The Huntington Library in southern California also had a bootleg copy of the scroll photographs that made the Cave 4 editors nervous. The Huntington had acquired its photos from philanthropist Elizabeth Hays Bechtel, who had financed a rephotographing of the scrolls in 1980 on behalf of the Ancient Biblical Manuscript

Center in Claremont, California. Though the new photos were duly deposited, Bechtel had a falling out with the center and had a private microfilm of the scrolls made for herself. Before her death in 1987, she gave the microfilm to the Huntington.

In August, Eugene Ulrich wrote to the library asking that they give their photos to the Ancient Biblical Manuscript Center, one of two official American depositories of scroll photos. (Hebrew Union College in Cincinnati is the other.) The library balked, and while Wacholder, Abegg, and Eisenman toiled on their publications, library director William Moffett began to wonder if he should release the scroll microfilm.

The Rediscovery of the Scrolls

In the end, the race was won by the computer. Abegg finished inputting all of the texts toward the end of August. Wacholder and Abegg's first volume of reconstructed transcriptions—containing some fragments of the *Damascus Document* and some other texts—was ready for publication. Shanks announced in a press conference on September 4 the publication of *A Preliminary Edition of the Unpublished Dead Sea Scrolls, Fascicle One*. In the book's foreword Shanks wrote,

> This is a historic book. A hundred years from now this book will still be cited—not only on account of its scholarship, but because it broke the monopoly on the still-unpublished Dead Sea Scrolls.[28]

The news became the lead story for most major newspapers and national TV broadcasts. The front page of the *New York Times*, adopting Shanks's phraseology, used the headline COMPUTER BREAKS MONOPOLY ON STUDY OF DEAD SEA SCROLLS (Sept. 5). The *Washington Post* preferred the racier RENEGADES BRING DEAD SEA SCROLLS TO LIGHT (Sept. 5). Some newspapers followed with editorials praising the action, often echoing Shanks's editorials in *BAR*. The Cave 4 team was always pejoratively described as a "cartel" or a "coterie," and little effort was made to examine the other side of the question, or even to grasp what exactly had happened—for, of course, the Dead Sea Scrolls themselves had not been published, but simply reconstructions of tentative transcriptions.

Biblical scholars, more aware of the history of the problem and of the complex issues involved, nevertheless tended to divide into two camps—those who supported and those who opposed the bootleg publication. Not all of those opposing the move were insiders, or friends of insiders. Many simply had qualms about the honorability of what was, in essence, the utilization of someone else's work. Wacholder and Abegg had reconstituted, not made, the transcripts. Whatever the faults of the team, they had still done that work themselves, and for others to publish it under their own name was felt to be unjust.

Supporters of the publication felt, on the other hand, that the Cave 4 team had simply gotten what it deserved for its arrogance, its secrecy, and its long dereliction of duty. Still others, neither pro nor con, had reservations about the accuracy of the publication; and even those who granted that it might be accurate still fretted about the continuing lack of photos to corroborate the readings. But almost everyone, whatever his opinion, pored eagerly over the texts.

The debate did not have long to gather steam before another bomb was dropped: On September 22, the Huntington Library, emboldened by the "computer texts," finally announced that it would allow all qualified scholars access to its collection of Dead Sea Scrolls photographs. This was instantly recognized as a decision of far greater import than the release of the transcriptions. It meant the end of the Cave 4 team's control of the photos.

Although the Huntington was not contractually bound to honor the IAA's restricted-access policy, General Drori threatened to sue the Huntington for "both a breach of contract and of ethics." The Huntington's director, William Moffett, replied,

> We're not party to that contract. It has nothing to do with us. . . . No damage has been done to anyone by providing access. We are calling on the Israel Department of Antiquities [sic] to join with us in the spirit of intellectual freedom and not to impose further barriers to scholarship.[29]

The IAA backed away from any legal action against the Huntington, and eventually, bowing to the inevitable, announced on October 27 that it would allow unrestricted access to the official photos of the scrolls, providing that no one outside the team would publish their findings.

Finally, on November 25, Emanuel Tov announced that that last restriction would also be lifted. Anyone could now look at the photos and publish in full what they read there. The IAA authorized a full publication of over 6,400 photos on microfiche—ironically, through the same Dutch publisher that had cancelled the publication of Eisenman's secret photos.[30] The Dead Sea Scrolls had finally emerged from their last hiding place.

"A Good Time for Scholars"

Although the Dead Sea Scrolls were liberated, bitter controversies continued to rage. Less than a week before Tov lifted all restrictions on access and publication, Hershel Shanks published Eisenman's collection of scroll photos. Eisenman, who had hoped to be the first to break the cartel, was bringing up the rear. But *A Facsimile Edition of the Dead Sea Scrolls* did become the means by which most scholars actually had their first look at the unpublished texts.

As with Wacholder and Abegg's book, Eisenman and Robinson's book of photos had its share of critics. Many (including Eisenman and Robinson) found Shanks's self-congratulatory foreword in bad taste. (It was dropped in the second edition.) More importantly, the reproduction of many photos was poor, so that a number of fragments could not be read. Finally, some scholars felt that the publication of the photos was unethical. Stephen A. Kaufman, a professor at Hebrew Union College, wrote:

> The thousands of mostly tiny [scroll] fragments did not mount themselves. The arrangements reflect, rather, tens of thousands of hours of scholarly efforts to make sense out of an enormously complicated jigsaw puzzle. The photographs themselves are useless without the thousands of hours of scholarship that have gone into the preparation of several different stages of "catalogues" of their contents, primarily by Elisha Qimron, John Strugnell, and, most recently, Stephen A. Reed. . . . The efforts of all these scholars, as well as those who participated in the preparation of the concordance, were directed towards ultimate publication, not obfuscation. To publish their work without permission is theft, pure and simple![31]

Kaufman went on to say that outsiders should wait until 1997—the deadline announced by the IAA for publication of all the *DJD* volumes—before proceeding with their own publications of the scrolls. It seems safe to say that few will follow this advice.

In November 1991, thousands of scholars met in Kansas City for the annual meeting of the Society of Biblical Literature, the largest organization of biblical scholars in the United States. An overflow crowd came to a panel discussion on the Dead Sea Scrolls, where Abegg, Ulrich, Tov, Moffett, and others shared the stage. Calls for harmony were the order of the day; it was here that Tov announced the lifting of all restrictions on access and publication. Ulrich admitted that the Cave 4 publication project as set up in 1953 was "partly flawed and problematic" and hoped that the new access to the Dead Sea Scrolls would foster "not anger, not jealousy, and not sensationalism" but "trust, harmony, and cooperation."[32]

Whether these virtues are realized in future scholarship on the Dead Sea Scrolls is still an open question. Although many hope for an era of peace and are actively working for it, some team members are still bitter about the way things unfolded. In January 1992, Elisha Qimron sued Shanks for publishing a bootleg transcription of 4QMMT in the *Facsimile Edition*. In March 1993, an Israeli court awarded Qimron 100,000 shekels (more than $40,000) in damages for breach of copyright and "mental anguish"—far less than the 472,500 shekels ($250,000) requested, but establishing the right of scholarly copyright over reconstructed scrolls.[33] Qimron also threatened action against Wacholder and Abegg if they published "his" text in volume 3 of their *Preliminary Edition*. As this book goes to press, Wacholder and Abegg were considering taking legal action against Qimron before publishing more of their reconstituted texts.

A similar flap occurred a year after the Kansas City meeting. In November of 1992 Eisenman and Wise published *The Dead Sea Scrolls Uncovered*, containing transcriptions and translations of fifty scroll texts. Although many of these texts had already been published, the subtitle of the book ("The First Complete Translation and Interpretation of 50 Key Documents Withheld for Over 35 Years") suggested that all the texts were new. Furthermore, many of the former "insider" scholars accused Eisenman and Wise of using their work, published and unpublished, without proper credit. Wise, who had been mainly responsible for the transcriptions and translations, admitted to careless documentation in the book and apologized in a statement delivered at a conference on the scrolls in New York in December. The scholars accepted Wise's apology and retracted their accusations.

Although harmony was restored, the conflict exposed the ongoing rancor that remains in the field of Qumran study. Norman Golb of the University of Chicago claimed that the fight revealed "a continuous resistance to the principle of open access to the scrolls."[34]

That was specious; access was no longer an issue. But proper credit for work done—the material from which scholarly reputations are built—is still a touchy subject. Despite Qimron's legal victory, there are unresolved legal and ethical questions over the degree to which a scholar may claim ownership in the reading and publishing of an ancient text.

But peacefully or with bitterness, it is certainly true overall, as Emanuel Tov noted in *BAR,* that "it is a good time for the scrolls. It is a good time for scholars."[35] The team—it has now grown to include fifty-three members—continues to work on publishing its official edition before the turn of the century. Fourteen scrolls arrived in the United States in 1993 for exhibitions at the Library of Congress and the New York Public Library. Technical studies continue to be published, and many books for a popular audience are coming out. The Dead Sea Scrolls, forty-five years out of their caves, have been rediscovered.

Perhaps the best summary of these events is found in the words of Scripture, as applied by Emanuel Tov. Tov had been one of Abegg's teachers when Abegg studied in Israel. When Tov first encountered his former student at the Kansas City meeting, he quoted to him in Hebrew the words of Isaiah 1:2: *banim giddalti v'romamti* ("I reared children and brought them up"). He meaningfully left the second half of the verse for Abegg to supply: *v'hem pash'u bi:* "But they have rebelled against me."

Notes

1. William Dever, quoted in the *New York Times,* 7 January 1973, 18.

2. J. A. Sanders, "Palestinian Manuscripts 1947–1972," in *Qumran and the History of the Biblical Text,* ed. Frank Moore Cross and Shemaryahu Talmon (Cambridge, Mass.: Harvard University Press, 1975), 401–2.

3. Vermes's mention of the Bar Kokhba documents is a useful reminder that the Cave 4 team had no monopoly on slowness in publication. The Bar Kokhba documents, discovered in two locations in the

Judean wilderness, had been in Israeli hands since 1960. Most of them have still not been published.

4. Geza Vermes, *The Dead Sea Scrolls: Qumran in Perspective,* rev. ed. (Philadelphia: Fortress, 1981; originally published 1977), 23–24.

5. The *Biblical Archaeologist,* which is published by the American Schools of Oriental Research (ASOR), should not be confused with the similarly titled *Biblical Archaeology Review.*

6. David Noel Freedman, "Letter to the Readers," *Biblical Archaeologist* 40/2 (September 1977): 96–97. Despite Freedman's *mea culpa,* the Leviticus Scroll from Cave 11 was not published until 1985.

7. Patrick Skehan, "4QLXXNum: A Pre-Christian Reworking of the Septuagint," *Harvard Theological Review* 70 (1977): 39–50. Cross did allow some of his graduate students to use the texts from his lot in their research, as for instance, in Eugene Ulrich's *Qumran Text of Samuel and Josephus* (1978). In this way, at least partial information about the unpublished biblical texts was released. Later Cross allowed some of his students to produce preliminary editions of his texts for their dissertations.

8. Strugnell to author, 14 February 1992.

9. Benoit's remarks were published in *Revue Biblique* 90 (1983): 97–100, in the course of reviewing John Trever's revision of his book, titled in that edition *The Dead Sea Scrolls: A Personal Account.* Trever, who ought to have known better, had echoed some of Allegro's remarks about the Catholic makeup of the team. Benoit was also annoyed by an absurd article ("Whatever Happened to the Dead Sea Scrolls?" by Martin Larson) in the *Journal of Historical Review,* an organ of a "Holocaust revisionist" group, which had accused the "Zionist-Israeli regime" of engineering a cover-up of the Qumran material.

10. Geza Vermes, in a review of *DJD* 7, in the *Journal of Jewish Studies* 35 (1984): 86–87.

11. Geza Vermes, "Introductory Remarks," *Journal of Jewish Studies* 39 (1988): 4.

12. John Strugnell, "The Qumran Scrolls: A Report on Work in Progress," in *Jewish Civilization in the Hellenistic Period,* ed. S. Talmon (Philadelphia: Trinity Press, 1991), 104–6.

13. Ulrich to author, 28 September 1992.

14. The Dead Sea Scrolls are referred to by cave number, location, and then either by number or some other abbreviation. Thus 4QMMT refers to Cave 4 (4) from Qumran (Q), the text known as MMT (from a Hebrew phrase serving as title: *Miqsat Maasei ha-Torah,* "Some Matters of the Law" or "Some Works of the Law"). For more on this text, see pp. 113–16.

15. Strugnell to author, 14 December 1992.

16. Quoted in *Biblical Archaeological Review* (September/October 1989): 20.

17. Robert Eisenman, "The Desecration of the Scrolls," *Midstream* (December 1991): 15.

18. Eisenman says today that he was not responsible for distributing the pirated transcription of 4QMMT, as stated in *The Dead Sea Scrolls Deception,* 78. He argues that Strugnell and his Israeli collaborator, Elisha Qimron, had distributed the transcription to their students and that one of these copies had been passed around and reproduced. This account seems accurate.

19. Baigent and Leigh quote Eisenman as saying, "I decided to circulate anything that came into my hands without conditions. This was the service I could render: plus, it would undermine the international cartel or monopoly of such documents" (*The Dead Sea Scrolls Deception,* 78).

20. Text quoted from "The Mogilany Resolution 1989: Minutes of a Meeting of Participants of the Dead Sea Scrolls Colloquium (Mogilany, 14 September 1989)," *The Qumran Chronicle* 1 (Cracow, Poland), (August 1990): 10.

21. A popular guess has been that the pictures come from Najib Albina, the official photographer of the Palestine Archaelogical Museum during the period of Jordanian rule (see Joseph Fitzmyer, *Responses to 101 Questions on the Dead Sea Scrolls* [New York: Paulist, 1992], 157). Eisenman says unequivocally that the pictures did not come from Albina or anyone connected with him (to author, 12 October 1992).

22. Wise to author, 28 September 1992.

23. Later in the year, Strugnell foolishly referred to Geza Vermes as "incompetent" (Philip E. Ross, "Overview: Dead Sea Scrolls," *Scientific American* [November 1990]: 38).

24. There are unexplained discrepancies between the Hebrew and English versions. For example, the "horrible religion" remark appears only in the English version.

25. The concordance was not "secret," as Shanks later claimed. De Vaux clearly acknowledged its existence in the introduction to *DJD* 6, 7.

26. Abegg to author, 9 June 1992. All further quotations from Abegg are from this interview.

27. Eisenman to author, 12 October 1992.

28. Shanks, "Foreword," *A Preliminary Edition of the Unpublished Dead Sea Scrolls, Fascicle One* (Washington, D.C.: Biblical Archaeology Society, 1991), vii.

29. The quotations are drawn from stories in the *Los Angeles Times,* 23–24 September 1991.

30. *The Dead Sea Scrolls on Microfiche,* edited by Tov and Stephen Pfann, was finally published in April 1993.

31. Stephen A. Kaufman, "The Ethical Issues: A Position Statement," *Comprehensive Aramaic Lexicon Newsletter* 9 (February 1992): 5.

32. A report on the Dead Sea Scrolls session appears in Eugene Lovering, "SBL News: In Dead Sea Scrolls Session, SBL Issues a Statement on Access to Written Materials," *Religious Studies News* 7/1 (January 1992): 3–5.

33. See A. Landau, "The Dead Sea Scrolls and the Recognized Rules of Copyright," *Jerusalem Post,* 3 April 1993, 8; Shanks, "Paying the Price

for Freeing the Scrolls," *Biblical Archaeology Review* 19 (July/August 1993): 65–68.

34. Quoted in Ellen Coughlin, "Book Reopens Wounds in Battle Over Access to Dead Sea Scrolls," *Chronicle of Higher Education* (6 January 1993): A10.

35. E. Tov, "Expanded Team of Editors Hard at Work on Variety of Texts," *Biblical Archaeological Review* 18 (July/August 1992): 75.

Chapter 5

Who Wrote the Scrolls?

There is something in the study of the Dead Sea Scrolls that tempts outsiders to describe its practitioners as mad. Literary critic Stanley Edgar Hyman wrote in 1957 that the books he had read on the subject reminded him of "a Sunday outing on the madhouse lawn, with everyone mumbling his own fancies and no one listening to anyone else." He went on to describe, somewhat hysterically, "the shifting figures of theory dancing in the shadows, and the animal growlings of passion and prejudice. Out there you venture at your peril."[1]

Decades later, journalist Ron Rosenbaum, writing in *Vanity Fair* (of all places), spoke of the scrolls' "extraordinary power to haunt, obsess, and torment those who sought to divine their meaning."[2] Rosenbaum's blurb writer wrote even more sensationally that "Scholars, mystics, and Messiah freaks have been driven mad searching for the fingerprints of God in the Dead Sea Scrolls."

Academics who know anything about the study of the Qumran documents will not be able to resist a smile at such florid descriptions of their trade. Journalists are drawn to loud voices and passionate personalities, and Qumran studies have had their share of both. And some scholars—John Allegro, for example—have been unable to resist the urge to go public with ideas that their academic peers have found unworthy of serious consideration.

By contrast, serious scroll scholars have—and still do—put forth mutually incompatible theories about the scrolls with heated certainty. Laypeople who wander into this kind of academic crossfire may well wonder if there is not something a little strange about an area of study where people can't agree on some of the most basic facts. For instance, it may seem peculiar that there is currently a lively dispute about who wrote the scrolls.

Actually, the question "Who wrote the scrolls?" needs some explanation. There were three types of texts found among the Dead Sea Scrolls: books of the Old Testament, nonbiblical religious books previously known, and nonbiblical religious books previously unknown. The last type of writing is the one that makes people ask, "Where did they come from? Whose ideas are these? What group is responsible for this literature?"

Among these unknown writings there is a unity of outlook and expression that makes one want to see them as the product of a single group. The *War Scroll,* for instance, speaks of a war that will break out at the end of time between the "Sons of Light" and the "Sons of Darkness." The *Manual of Discipline* also speaks of the "Sons of Light" and the "Sons of Darkness," and explains that light and darkness are the two ways that God has appointed for man to walk in. Those who are chosen to be "Sons of Light" are guided by the "Spirit of Light," while the "Sons of Darkness" are correspondingly under the control of the "Spirit of Darkness." The rest of the *Manual* describes the entrance requirements and rules for living of a certain community that has made a covenant to live in accordance with all of God's laws, "to love all the sons of light . . . and to hate all the sons of darkness."

The *Manual,* in turn, has many rules and turns of phrase in common with the *Damascus Document,* which describes a group that has entered "a new covenant in the land of Damascus." This "Damascus" group, according to the *Damascus Document,* owed its formation to an unnamed "Teacher of Righteousness." This Teacher along with the community is said to have struggled against a "congregation of traitors" who was led by a man, also unnamed, but variously called the Man of Mockery, the Preacher of Falsehood, or the Man of Falsehood.

The *Habakkuk Pesher* also refers to the Teacher of Righteousness, the Man of the Lie, and the Congregation of Traitors, and we are introduced to another villain, the Wicked Priest, who persecuted the Teacher. We hear of a warlike people, the Kittim, also mentioned in the *War Scroll*. Finally, in the *Thanksgiving Scroll*, we have some poems in which the speaker gives thanks to God for helping him against "traitors" and "liars" and for giving him the privilege of revealing God's truth as an "interpreter of wonderful mysteries." These psalms seem to have been written by (or for) the Teacher himself.

In short, these writings all seem to have their source in one particular Jewish sect. But it will be plain from the sketchy description just given that they were frustratingly averse to speaking plainly. They never named their enigmatic Teacher or his opponents; more importantly, they never named themselves. They used a hundred descriptions for their group, mostly laudatory—the sons of light, the congregation of the righteous, those who have entered the covenant, the community of God, and so on—but no recurring identifying label.

It was obviously important to scholars to try to decide who this group was. To do that it was necessary to know where in history to look for such a group. Most scholars had already narrowed down the search to one particular period of Jewish history: the second century B.C. to the first century A.D.

The most decisive argument was based on paleography. A carbon-14 test also weakly supported the timespan. By measuring the rate of decay of the carbon-14 atom found in all organic matter, scientists can roughly determine the time of origin of any organic substance. A technician at the University of Chicago performed a carbon-14 test on a flaxen cloth covering that one of the Cave 1 scrolls was wrapped in. (The cloth was chosen because the tested substance had to be reduced to carbon, that is burned.) According to the test, the cloth originated in A.D. 33, with a margin of error of two hundred years—not a very exact result! But it does exclude the possibility of modern forgery and allows the paleographical estimate to stand (see further, pp. 142–43).

Another line of evidence the early Qumran scholars used was the pottery found in the caves. Archaeologists can tell as much from pottery as paleographers can from a handwritten text. In fact, it is easier for the archaeologist, who has more materials to work with, for wherever ancient people lived, they left behind lots of pottery. Pottery types changed over time just as writing styles did, and therefore they can be dated with precision. The pottery found in some of the caves, although containing some unique types, fit into the general period estimated by the paleographers.

Important evidence for dating was found in the scrolls themselves. Although they do not mention many historical figures by name (other than ones from the Old Testament), the ones they do mention come from the second and first centuries B.C. Two kings from the period when the Greeks controlled the Holy Land are mentioned in the *Nahum Pesher* from Cave 4: "Antiochus," probably Antiochus IV Epiphanes, who reigned from 175 to 164 B.C., and "Demetrius," apparently Demetrius III (95–87 B.C.). The calendaric text called *Mishmarot* ("Priestly Courses") mentions names from the Hasmonean period, when Jewish priest-kings ruled a more or less independent Judea: "John," "Shelomzion," and "Hyrcanus," referring to, respectively, John Hyrcanus, who ruled Judea from 134 to 104 B.C., Queen Salome Alexandra (76–67 B.C.), and one of Salome's sons, Hyrcanus II (67 B.C.). The name "Aemilius" appears twice. Aemilius Scaurus was the Roman governor of the province of Syria after the Romans took over the government of Syria-Palestine. A recently published hymn mentions "Jonathan the King," either Jonathan (160–142 B.C.) or Alexander Jannaeus (103–76 B.C.).[3]

The first generation of scroll scholars, therefore, had to use several different kinds of circumstantial evidence, from sources outside the scrolls, to get a fix on the origin and nature of this group. The earliest, most commonly advanced, and still most widely held theory is that the scroll sectarians were a group called the Essenes.

The Essene Hypothesis

According to the Jewish historian Flavius Josephus, writing in the first century A.D., the Essenes were one of three principal sects of Judaism in the first two centuries B.C., the others being the Pharisees and Sadducees. Unlike the other two, the Essenes are not mentioned in the New Testament, but Josephus describes them in much greater detail than he does the others.

In his book *The Jewish War,* which deals with the Jewish revolt against Rome from A.D. 66 to 70, Josephus gives a rich and admiring description of the Essenes. He mentions several intriguing features: They abstain from marriage. They despise riches and hold all their goods in common. They appoint overseers to govern their common affairs. There are groups of Essenes in every city of Israel. They wear white garments. They pray every day at sunrise. They meet for the noon and evening meals after purifying themselves in cold water. They maintain orderly speech in their meetings. They strictly obey their superiors. They avoid swearing. They study ancient writings. They are stricter than the other Jews in observing the Sabbath. They require new members to undergo a lengthy period of probation. They believe in the immortality of the soul.

Elsewhere in *The Jewish War* and in his later work, *The Antiquities of the Jews,* Josephus stresses that the Essenes are strongly predestinarian, believing that all things are determined beforehand by God.

Another ancient writer who admired the Essenes was the Jewish philosopher Philo, who lived in Egypt and was an older contemporary of Josephus. In his book *Every Good Man Is Free,* Philo uses the Essenes as examples of the freedom of men who have learned to control themselves and their passions. His description of the Essenes agrees in most points with Josephus, adding that they abstain from war, do not engage in commerce, do not offer sacrifices, and own no slaves.

There are some obvious similarities between the Essenes and the sect of the Dead Sea Scrolls. According to the *Manual of Discipline,* the Qumran sect also required its new members to give up their worldly goods to be held in common by the group. And like the Essenes, they had a strict hierarchy, ate communal meals, and studied ancient writings. They maintained orderly speech in their meetings: Josephus says, "They give every one leave to speak in their turn" (*War* II.viii.5); the *Manual* says, "Let no one interrupt his neighbor before he finishes speaking. . . . the one who is asked (to speak) shall speak in his turn" (VI,10–11).

The initiation procedure is also very similar. According to Josephus,

> If any one has a mind to come over to their sect, he is not immediately admitted, but he is prescribed the same method of living which they use for a year, while he continues excluded. . . . And when he has given evidence, during that time, that he can observe their continence, he approaches nearer to their way of living, and is made a partaker of the waters of purification; yet is he not even now admitted to live with them; for after this demonstration of his fortitude, his temper is tried two more years; and if he appear to be worthy, they then admit him into their society. (*War* II.viii.7).[4]

A similar routine is outlined in the *Manual:*

> The Overseer shall examine in front of the Many any one of Israel who is willing to be joined to the Congregation of the Community as to his mind and his deeds; and if he is fit for the regimen, the overseer shall bring him into the covenant to return to the truth and to turn aside from all evil; and he shall teach him all the ways of the Community. And afterwards, when he comes to stand before the Many, everyone may ask questions about his affairs. . . . When he draws near to the Congregation of the Community, he shall not touch the Purity [the food] of the Many [share the communal meal] until they shall examine him as to his spirit and deeds after he has fulfilled one year. And also let him not mingle with the Many. When he has fulfilled a year in the Community, the Many shall ask about his affairs. . . . [If he is admitted], let him not touch the drink of the Many until he has fulfilled a second year in the Community (VI,13–21).

Although there are some differences between these accounts—Josephus appears to have left out one stage of the procedure—they clearly are describing the same process.

Like the Essenes, the Qumran sect was predestinarian. In the *Damascus Document,* God is said to destroy the wicked without remnant, "because God has not chosen them from of old; and before they were born he knew their deeds" (II,7–8). In the *Manual of Discipline* we read that "from the God of knowledge is everything that exists and comes into being; and before they are he has established their design. When they come into being at their time, they fulfill their task in accord with the design of his glory, and no one can change it" (III,15–16). In the *Thanksgiving Scroll* the poet praises the God of creation: "In the wisdom of thy knowledge thou hast established their time, ere ever they were" (I,19).

The parallels just mentioned are not exhaustive. One recent

author counts twenty-seven parallels in all between Josephus and the scrolls, and twenty-one more probable parallels, with only six discrepancies (about which more will be said later).[5]

One final crucial bit of lore about the Essenes comes from the Roman writer Pliny. In his book *Natural History* he gives an account of the land of Palestine. He mentions the Essenes, describing their celibate communal lifestyle in tones of amazement. But he also notes that the Essenes lived on the western bank of the Dead Sea.

This fact alone—that the Essenes had a settlement on the western bank of the Dead Sea—was enough to start scholars speculating, even before any of them had been published, that the scrolls were Essene documents.[6] Sukenik quickly formed the hypothesis that the scrolls were Essene, and William Brownlee of the original ASOR group came to the same conclusion. The first press release about the scrolls, in April 1948, suggested that the *Manual of Discipline* may have been the work of Essenes.

The most influential advocate of the Essene view was the French scholar André Dupont-Sommer. He urged the Essene connection as early as 1949, and in a book published in 1950—before more than a few columns had been published of the *Manual,* the *War Scroll,* or the *Thanksgiving Scroll*—he pressed the identification and then continued to do so in later publications.[7] By the time all the Cave 1 scrolls had been published (1955), most scholars were persuaded that the Essenes had written the Dead Sea Scrolls. It remains the majority view today.

Solving the Mystery of the Teacher

The identification of the scroll-writing group is only one angle of Qumran research. Scholars have also attempted to decode the mysterious historical allusions in some of the texts and to link them up with the history of the sect. Although the Essene hypothesis does not stand or fall with any particular decoding, it has usually been aligned with the "Hasmonean" interpretation of the three main "characters" of the texts: the Wicked Priest, the Teacher of Righteousness, and the Man of the Lie.

According to the *Habakkuk Pesher,* the Wicked Priest was "called according to the name of truth at the beginning of his service, but when he had ruled in Israel, his heart became proud and he forsook God and betrayed the commandments for wealth" (VIII,9–11). He "gathered the wealth of the violent men who had rebelled against God, taking the wealth of the Gentiles" (VIII,11–12); he also "polluted the temple of God" (XII,8–9). His fate was to be "smitten with the judgments of wickedness; they wrought on him the horrors of evil diseases, acts of vengeance in the body of his flesh" (IX,1–2). The "cup of God's wrath destroys him" (XI,14–15). God "has given him into the power of his enemies to humiliate him with a plague to destruction in bitterness of soul, because he did evil to his chosen" (IX,10–11). The *Psalms Pesher* says that "God will pay him back by putting him into the power of the cruel Gentiles to pass judgment on him" (IV,9–10).

Scholars have struggled for years to identify this unsavory character with a historical figure. Most believe the Wicked Priest must have been one of the Hasmonean priestly rulers of Judea from 160 to 63 B.C., after the Maccabean rebellion. The period corresponds to the generally accepted date of the Dead Sea Scrolls, and only someone who was simultaneously a priest and a ruler could be said to have "ruled in Israel" or be in a position to "rob the Gentiles."

Only one of the Hasmoneans, the high priest Jonathan (160–142 B.C.), is recorded to have been killed by Gentiles, making him one of the most popular guesses for the Wicked Priest.[8] Jonathan conducted several successful military campaigns against the Greeks and other non-Jews and thus could easily have "taken the wealth of the Gentiles." He led the armies of Israel successfully before he accepted appointment as high priest—under the auspices of a Greek king!—which the sectarians might well have considered highly irregular, "betraying the commandments for the sake of wealth."

Two other items support the candidacy of Jonathan as the Wicked Priest. According to de Vaux, the settlement at Khirbet Qumran probably began sometime in the second half of the second century B.C. and therefore possibly during the reign of Jonathan. Also, Josephus first mentions the Essenes in his account of the reign of Jonathan (*Antiquities* XIII.v.9). If Jonathan was the Wicked Priest, then he persecuted the Teacher of Righteousness and his followers sometime between 160 and 142 B.C., the period of

Jonathan's priesthood. That gives us a firm date for the activity of the Teacher and the founding of the sect.

The *Habakkuk Pesher* describes the Teacher in glowing terms as that "Priest in whose heart God has put understanding to interpret all the words of his servants the prophets" (II,8–9) and as one to whom "God made known all the secrets of the words of his servants the prophets" (VII,4–5). This inspired man gathered around himself a circle of followers, was persecuted by the Wicked Priest—perhaps because of "the instruction [torah] that he [the Teacher] sent to him" (*Psalms Pesher* IV, 8)—may have been exiled (XI,6), but was delivered from the danger of death by God's power (*Psalms Pesher* IV,9–10). Later he was peacefully "gathered in" (*Damascus Document* XIX,35).

If the *Thanksgiving Scroll* comes from the Teacher, then he was a man acutely conscious of being a sinner.

> I am a clay pot, compounded of water, a shameful secret, a fountain of filth, a caldron of iniquity, a figure of sin, an erring and perverse spirit, without understanding, fearful of righteous judgment (I,21–23).

And yet:

> You have made me a standard for the Chosen Ones of Righteousness, a knowledgeable interpreter of wonderful mysteries, to examine men of truth and to test those who love instruction (II,13–14).

What "wonderful mysteries" was the Teacher custodian of? We do not know exactly the extent of his teaching. It evidently included some esoteric knowledge of God's hidden plan; the teaching about the division between light and darkness and divine predestination to one of these realms is basic to the sect's consciousness. They also had a vivid and detailed script of the final events of the age and their own place in it (*War Scroll*). They expected a divine intervention in history, restoring Israel to its privileged place in the world, with the sect as the kernel of the new Israel and the source of its purified priesthood. The sect kept a high ethical code that entailed "doing the good and the right before him as he commanded by Moses and all his servants the prophets, loving all that he has chosen and hating all that he has rejected" (*Manual of Discipline* I,3–4). They also observed a rigid version of the Jewish law that called for a strict separation from all nonmembers (4QMMT, the *Temple Scroll*).

Although scholars basically agree on the Hasmonean origin of the Wicked Priest, there is little or no agreement on the identity of the Teacher. Indeed, it is uncommon for scholars to suggest a particular historical person as the Teacher, because, in contrast to the Priest, he was not a public figure.

The third major figure of this story is the "Man of the Lie," also called the "Man of Mockery." Although he was originally taken to be the same as the Wicked Priest, it is generally accepted today that the Man of the Lie is someone else entirely. According to the *Habakkuk Pesher,* he "rejected the Law in the midst of the whole congregation" (V,11–12); this event somehow involved a "rebuke of the Teacher of Righteousness" (V,10). We also read that he "led many astray to build a vain city in bloodshed" (X,9–10); similarly, he "led many astray with lying words, because they had chosen easy things and did not listen to the Knowledgeable Interpreter [another name for the Teacher]" (*Psalms Pesher* I,18–19).

Most scholars believe that these vague clues point to a schismatic teacher within the sect. Proposing a different (more lenient?) interpretation of the law from that of the Teacher, he led out a sizable faction from the original group. We know nothing more about him, although the crisis he brought on the sect must have been even more traumatic than the Priest's attack. The *Damascus Document* does not mention the Wicked Priest, but alludes bitterly to the "Man of Mockery" and the "congregation of traitors."

After the Teacher's death, the history of the sect was described in vague terms in the *Damascus Document.*

> In the Age of Wrath, 390 years after he [God] put them [Israel] into the power of Nebuchadnezzar king of Babylon, he visited them and made to grow from Israel and from Aaron a root of planting to inherit his land to grow fat on the goodness of the soil. And they discerned their iniquity and they knew that they were guilty men. They were as blind men and as those who grope for the way for 20 years. Then God discerned their deeds, that they had sought him with a whole heart; so he raised up for them a Teacher of Righteousness to guide them in the way of his heart (I,5–11).

Scholars have thoroughly discussed the scant information present in this passage since the *Damascus Document* was published in 1910, and especially since the discovery of the scrolls. The plain meaning of the text is that 390 years after the fall of Jerusalem in 586 B.C.—that is, in or around 196 B.C.—God established a community to be the faithful remnant of Israel. After twenty years of serving God faithfully but ignorantly, God gave them the Teacher to guide them. That would be around 176 B.C.

Obviously the Teacher could have lived on into the reign of Jonathan if his ministry began around 176. Many scholars, however, wish to fix the beginning of the Teacher's activity at the foundation of Khirbet Qumran, and 176 B.C. is too early for that. Hence there is a tendency among scroll scholars to explain away the figures in the *Damascus Document* as symbolic, metaphorical, or approximate.

It is increasingly common with some scholars, however, to take the figures literally. And there is no real reason to interlock the beginning of the Teacher's ministry with the foundation of the settlement (assuming that Khirbet Qumran is the site of the sect's activity, which is also under question). A synthesis of all these details produced a religious group (Essenes?) beginning in the early second century B.C., which gained momentum under the Teacher twenty years later, endured persecution under Jonathan in the mid-second century, founded a settlement at Qumran toward the end of that century, and continued as a viable body that produced (or collected) a sizable library until its end in the Jewish War of A.D. 66–70. Such a synthesis would be consistent, reasonable, and coherent.

Nevertheless, there are many loose ends and uncertainties. The identification of the Priest with Jonathan is not accepted by all; Jonathan's career, as it is presented in Josephus and in 1 Maccabees, is almost purely military. There is no indication that he would have any interest in or motive for persecuting any faction of Jews. The Jewish state was too fragile at the time for internecine disputes. Cross favors another Hasmonean ruler, Jonathan's younger brother Simon.[9] The high-priesthood was given to Simon and his descendants in perpetuity in 140 B.C. He is therefore more likely to have had trouble with dissident religious groups. But he was assassinated by his son-in-law, not killed by Gentiles. Other scholars see Alexander

Jannaeus as the Wicked Priest. If the dates in the *Damascus Document* are to be taken literally, however, Alexander's time (103–76 B.C.) is too late.

The difficulty in finding historical identifications for the Teacher and the Priest have led some to conclude that these designations do not refer to any one person. The "Teacher of Righteousness" is a name for whoever happens to be the leader of the sect at a given time. The "Wicked Priest" is whoever happens to be the ruling high priest. In this theory, the Wicked Priest who persecutes the Teacher is not necessarily the same Priest who is killed by the Gentiles. The Teacher who founded the sect does not have to be the one who was hounded to his "place of exile," and so on.[10] Although theories of this type have their appeal, it is hard not to feel that they are a kind of surrender in the face of difficulties.

Another loose end is that the *Damascus Document* identifies Damascus as the location of the sect. Since most researchers find it possible, and desirable, to understand the history and nature of the sect wholly in terms of the history of Israel, they wonder why they were said to be located in the city of Damascus. It is fairly common to understand the reference "Damascus" as symbolic. But symbolic of what? Cross takes "Damascus" to be the settlement at Khirbet Qumran, based on a sectarian reinterpretation of Amos 5:27 ("Therefore I will send you into exile beyond Damascus"). Others, like Jerome Murphy-O'Connor, take "Damascus" to be Babylon, where the Jews were exiled after the fall of Judah in 586 B.C. He develops an elaborate theory that envisions a Mesopotamian origin for the Essenes, who, on returning to Judah in the early second century B.C., recoiled from the prevalent immorality they found there. Shocked, they retreated into the desert and founded a community at Qumran; meanwhile a number of their brethren remained in Babylon.[11]

Neither of these suggestions is wholly convincing. "Damascus" as a name for Qumran is rather opaque, especially since the Bible verse on which it is supposedly based speaks of an exile *beyond* Damascus. As for "Damascus" being Babylon, why not simply call Babylon "Babylon"? As with the chronological data, the simplest thing is to take "Damascus" literally: The Syrian city apparently was a prominent center of sectarian activity, and indeed, travelers moved freely between Palestine and Damascus. The *Damascus Document* evidently formed the constitution of the "exiled" sectarians—those living in "camps" in foreign countries—while the *Manual of Discipline* had a similar function for the Palestinian faction. That would account for both the similarities and the differences between the *Manual* and the *Document*. That there was traffic between Damascus and Qumran is indirectly shown by the presence in Cave 4 of documents written in Nabatean, the Aramaic dialect used by the citizens of the Arabian kingdom in which Damascus lay.[12]

Despite the uncertainties of the historical reconstruction, most scholars today accept some form of the Essene hypothesis along with some form of the historical "decoding" just described. Those who reject the Essene hypothesis often reject the "Hasmonean interpretation" as well.

The Ruin and the Scrolls

A third approach to solving the mysteries of the Dead Sea Scrolls is to understand them in the light of archaeology. In the early days of scroll study, some scholars like Dupont-Sommer also pointed out that there was a well-known, but unexcavated ruin, near the north end of the Dead Sea, in the vicinity of the scroll caves. This ruin was Khirbet Qumran. As previously noted, de Vaux was ultimately persuaded to open an excavation at Qumran.

The idea that the Essenes lived at Qumran and wrote their scrolls there and later stored them in the caves has become part of conventional scholarly wisdom. Since the connection between the ruin and the scrolls has been recently questioned, it is necessary to explain exactly how de Vaux, the excavator of the ruin, made the link in the first place and what the implications of it are.

Before the Dead Sea Scrolls were discovered, others had noticed the ruin and speculated about it. One scholar thought it might be the remains of a Roman fort, although the nearby cemetery with over a thousand graves made this dubious. But with the hundreds of ancient city mounds and large ruins in the Near East, no one had really considered this small site worth excavating.

De Vaux was intrigued by the possibility of learning more about the scrolls from the ruin and began excavating in 1951. He conducted archaeological campaigns there each year from 1953 to 1956, and the pottery and coins he found matched the period scholars had fixed as the time the Dead Sea Scrolls were written. Since the Qumran site was inhabited at the time the scrolls were written, and the scroll caves were all in the general vicinity of the site, and the Qumran sect seemed to be the Essenes, who according to Pliny, lived by the Dead Sea—what could be more plausible than to identify Khirbet Qumran with the Essene settlement?

De Vaux produced more evidence to support these general conclusions. His excavations revealed five different periods in the occupation of the site. The earliest occupation level dated from the eighth to the seventh centuries B.C., that is, from Old Testament times, long before the era of the scrolls. The next three levels, known as Periods Ia, Ib, and II, de Vaux dated from the second century B.C. to the first century A.D., the time of the Qumran sect. Period III, in de Vaux's opinion, represented a brief occupation of the site by a Roman garrison in the first century A.D., after the destruction of the buildings of Period II.

Of the mass of detail available about de Vaux's excavations,[13] only three points are of further relevance for our purposes: the evidence for the time of the beginning of the sectarian occupation, the evidence for its end, and the evidence that the scrolls were written there.

De Vaux believed that the beginning of Period Ia, and therefore the beginning of Essene occupation of the site, must have been towards the end of the second century B.C. His evidence is indirect. Period Ia is hardly distinguishable from Period Ib, but de Vaux thought he could detect modest building activity. Period Ib, on the other hand, saw a dramatic expansion of the structures on the site, with the enlargement of earlier buildings and the addition of gates, a tower, a kitchen, kilns, many cisterns, storerooms, workshops, and so on.[14] De Vaux dated the beginning of this period to the reign of Alexander Janneus (103–76 B.C.), due to the large number of coins minted from that king found in the level. Period Ia, then, must have begun before Alexander's reign—sometime in the second half of the second century B.C.

There was a gap in occupation between Ib and II lasting several decades, to judge from the coin evidence. The end of the sectarian occupation would be equivalent to the end of Period II. There is an unbroken series of coins from every ruler of Judea in Period II, beginning with Herod Archelaus (the son of Herod the

Great), who reigned from 4 B.C. to A.D. 6. In A.D. 66 the Jews, then in revolt against Roman rule, began minting their own money. Many coins minted in the first and second years of the revolt were found in Period II, but only a few from the third year of the revolt, A.D. 68. Then the coin series stops abruptly. The next coins found were from Period III, and they were Roman coins from the reign of Nero, also from the year A.D. 68. The difference in coins exactly coincides with the end of one period and the beginning of another.

De Vaux observed that a legion of the Roman army, according to Josephus, was in the vicinity of the Dead Sea in the summer of 68. He concluded that it was at this time that the Romans attacked the Qumran settlement and destroyed it.

> The Roman coins which begin in A.D. 67/68 do not *per se* prove that the Romans installed themselves at Khirbet Qumran in this same year, 68. But since these two groups of coins are distributed precisely between two successive levels, the Jewish coins certainly belonging to the lower level, that of the destruction, and the Roman coins certainly belonging to the level above this, the level of the reconstruction, it is reasonable to put forward the hypothesis that the year 68, at which the two numismatic sequences meet, marks the destruction of the lower level and the initiation of the higher one. And, since this explanation is in accordance with the historical data, it acquires that degree of certainty with which a historian of antiquity often has to be content. It is in this sense that I consider it certain that Khirbet Qumran was destroyed by the Romans in June 68 of our era.[15]

If the Dead Sea Scrolls were indeed written by the Qumran sect at Khirbet Qumran, then none of them could have been written after A.D. 68.

Was there any evidence that the scrolls were in fact written at Khirbet Qumran? De Vaux thought there was. In one of the rooms the excavators discovered some large chunks of mudbrick covered with smooth plaster. When these chunks were reassembled at the Palestine Archaeological Museum, they formed a long, low table about sixteen feet long but less than two feet high. The discovery of several inkwells in the same location led de Vaux to think the room was a scriptorium, a writing room, the table serving as a bench where scribes would spread out their scrolls to write on. In one scholar's words, "the identification of this room as the scriptorium effectively sealed the connection between the caves and the ruins, and thus understandably its discovery marked one of the high points of the excavation."[16]

But even if the scroll caves and the ruins were in fact connected, what of it? Only the scrolls themselves could give the details needed to identify its writers. And yet if the scroll writers lived at Khirbet Qumran, it would almost necessarily follow that they were Essenes.

> The scholar who would "exercise caution" in identifying the sect of Qumran with the Essenes places himself in an astonishing position; he must suggest seriously that two major parties each formed communistic religious communities in the same district of the desert of the Dead Sea and lived together in effect for two centuries, holding similar bizarre views, performing similar or rather identical lustrations, ritual meals, and ceremonies. Further, the scholar must suppose that one community, carefully described by classical authors, disappeared without building remains or even potsherds behind; while the other community, systematically ignored by the classical sources, left extensive ruins and even a great library.[17]

Clearly the Essene hypothesis, on the basis of the scrolls themselves, has a lot going for it. If the texts are connected to the ruins, the hypothesis becomes even more powerful. It is indeed difficult to imagine that a group living near the Dead Sea (like the Essenes) during the Hasmonean and Roman periods of Jewish history (when the Essenes lived) wrote books that remind one of the Essenes without in fact being the Essenes. This line of reasoning has proven so persuasive that in 1958 Millar Burrows wrote that "few [scholars] even acknowledge that the question is open for discussion."[18] One scholar was recently moved to say that the Essene hypothesis "now commands universal assent."[19]

But although the hypothesis is by far the most widely held, it does not have the field to itself, and in fact, the criticisms of it have increased in recent years. Virtually every component of the Essene theory as sketched above is now being rethought, and criticisms that had been considered shelved years ago are now surfacing.[20]

Objections to the Essene Theory

To Josephus, Philo, and Pliny, one of the most remarkable things about the Essenes was their repudiation of marriage. Pliny wondered how they lived "without women, sex, or money, with only palm trees for company" (*Natural History* 5/17). And yet the sectarian scrolls did not command celibacy, and a few passages presuppose that the sect members might be married. The *Damascus Document* says that their opponents had fallen into one of the devil's traps—i.e., "fornication, that is, to take two wives in their lifetime" (IV,21). Thus polygamy was forbidden, but not monogamy. Another passage acknowledges that sect members might want to get married and raise children (VII,7). Excavations in the cemetery of Khirbet Qumran uncovered the remains of a few women and children as well as men. If there were women at Qumran, and the sectarians were allowed to be married, how then could the sect be the Essenes?

Another discrepancy is the sect's attitude towards war. Philo says that the Essenes pursued only peaceful occupations and did not make any weapons of war, such as arrows, spears, swords, helmets, or armor—not even peaceful objects that could be used in war. And yet the *War Scroll* describes with relish the equipment and military tactics to be used by the "sons of light" against their enemies in the last days.

A third discrepancy is the sectarian attitude toward slaves. Philo and Josephus both agree that the Essenes rejected slavery: "There are no slaves among them, not a single one, but being free they help one another" (Philo, *Every Good Man,* 79). The *Damascus Document,* however, charges the sect member not to reprimand slaves on the Sabbath (XI,12) or to sell "his male or female slave to Gentiles, for they too have entered the covenant of Abraham" (XII,10–11).

If Josephus, Philo, and Pliny mention some typical characteristics of the Essenes that do not jibe with the Dead Sea Scroll sect, the scrolls themselves mention doctrines apparently unnoticed by the classical sources. One of the most important of these is the calendar used by the Qumran sect. Most groups in ancient Judaism, including the priestly establishment in charge of the temple services, used a calendar regulated by the phases of the moon, yielding a 354-day year. (Judaism still uses a lunar calendar.) But some groups, including the Dead Sea sect, used a 364-day solar calendar. One of the results of this deviation was that Jewish festivals consistently fell on different days for the sect than they did for the rest of the Jews.

That may be one reason the sect felt it necessary to separate themselves from the mainstream. The classical sources are completely silent about this important point.

Another feature of the sectarian scrolls absent from the classical sources is the importance of priests. The sect drew its members from "Israel and Aaron" (*Damascus Document* I,7; see also *Manual of Discipline* IX,11), that is, from laypeople and the priesthood; but the priesthood had preeminence:

> Only the sons of Aaron shall rule in justice and in wealth, and according to their mouth shall go forth the lot for every regulation of the men of the community and of the wealth of the holy men who walk blameless (*Manual* IX,7).

All of the other sectarian scrolls testify to the authority of the priests in the community. One might expect Josephus, who was himself of priestly descent and who claims to have studied with the Essenes as a youth, to say something about this, but he does not.

These examples illustrate how the description of the Essenes given in the classical sources and the account of the sect found in the Dead Sea Scrolls do not match up perfectly. There are places where both sources dovetail remarkably; there are also significant inconsistencies. Scholars have basically responded in three ways. The first is to find some way of reconciling the discrepancies with the Essene hypothesis. The second is to call the Qumran sect "Essene-like," "Essenic," or "Essenoid," but to stop short of identifying them outright with the Essenes. The third is to drop the Essenes out of the picture altogether and look for a group with a better fit.

The first group can point out that Josephus referred to a group of noncelibate Essenes.

> . . . there is another order of Essenes, who agree with the rest as to their way of living, and customs, and laws, but differ from them in the point of marriage, as thinking that by not marrying they cut off the principal part of human life, which is the prospect of succession; nay, rather, that if all men should be of the same opinion, the whole race of mankind would fail (*Jewish War* II.viii.13).

Perhaps the scrolls, or some of them, are the product of the "marrying Essenes." As for the female graves at Qumran, different explanations have been advanced: The women were unmarried females who looked after the young orphans raised by the sect; they were wives of the marrying Essenes; they were non-Essene children of fathers who converted to the sect after raising a family.[21] Finally, one could observe with some justification that the desolate marl terrace above the Dead Sea was no place to raise a family, especially since the Qumran ruins themselves turned up no living quarters of any size. Whatever the ideology of the group, it is unlikely that there were many family units living at Khirbet Qumran.

A similar tack can be taken to address the question of war. Although Philo mentions the Essenes' aversion to weapons of war, he stops short of calling them pacifists. Josephus, moreover, mentions a certain "John the Essene" as a participant in the revolt against the Romans. Finally, perhaps the *War Scroll* should not be taken too literally as a window into the daily life of the sect. It is a description of a war that is to occur at the end of time, when Israel as a whole joins the sect members in practicing righteousness, and together they all go to battle against the Gentiles and other "sons of darkness." It is not necessarily a reliable guide to the sectarians' day-to-day public behavior.

The discrepancy about slavery is a harder one to harmonize. The sources agree that the Essenes rejected slavery, yet the *Damascus Document* indicates that the sect did not. But one could resolve even this contradiction by pointing out that the *Damascus Document* was written for members living in "camps," an expression apparently used to denote sectarian cells within cities:

> This is the rule for the settlement in "camps." Those who walk in these rules in the time of wickedness until the appearance of the Messiah of Aaron and Israel shall be at least ten men. . . . No member of the "camps" shall have authority to bring in anyone to the congregation except by word of the overseer of the "camp" (*Damascus Document* XII,23–24, 12–13).

The *Manual of Discipline* (which does not mention slaves) could have been intended for the group at the "motherhouse" at Khirbet Qumran, while the *Damascus Document* (the only one to mention slaves) gave the rules for the necessarily different circumstances of the "town Essenes." Perhaps the "town Essenes" were the marrying and slaveholding ones, while the Qumran groups were the celibate ones without slaves. One problem with this otherwise plausible solution is that Josephus and Philo both say that the Essenes live in towns or villages; neither of them mention the Dead Sea settlement.

Their descriptions must apply to the town Essenes, since they know no other.

Those scholars who are unconvinced by these harmonizations but still find the Essene hypothesis appealing have to say that the Qumran sect is related to the Essenes, but not identical to the group that the classical sources describe. Millar Burrows belonged to this cautious group: "For the present it seems to me best not to speak of the Qumran sect as Essenes, but rather to say that the Essenes and the covenanters [members of the Qumran covenant], with other groups of which we know little or nothing, represented the same general type."[22]

Burrows's references to "groups of which we know little or nothing" is a worthwhile reminder that the Essenes, Pharisees, Sadducees, and Zealots—to name the most prominent ancient Jewish parties that the Qumran sect has been identified with—were not the only groups in the period under discussion. Early Christian writers mention Jewish sects like the Hemerobaptists, the Masbotheans, and the Sebueans. We know little about these sects besides their names. Not only that, but the roughly two hundred years between 150 B.C. and A.D. 68 allow for considerable changes to take place in all these sects. It is possible that the early Essenes (or whatever they were) differed from the later ones. Different scrolls were probably written at different points in the evolution of the sect.

In other words, it is possible, even likely, that we don't have all the information needed to identify the sect beyond the shadow of a doubt. This second group of scholars tends to emphasize these limits to our knowledge. And yet, as long as Khirbet Qumran is connected to the scrolls, Cross's objection to the "cautious" group, quoted above, is devastating. "If the people of the scrolls were not the Essenes," wrote Cross, "they were a similar sect, living in the same center, in the same era"[23]—so why not just call them Essenes and be done with it?

But there are those who find the Essene hypothesis, in its strong form or in its weaker "Essenoid" guise, totally unacceptable. They must be heard from next.

Notes

1. Stanley Edgar Hyman, "The Dead Sea Scrolls, or What You Will," *Commentary* 23 (1957): 570–71, 579.

2. Ron Rosenbaum, "Riddle of the Scrolls," *Vanity Fair* (November 1992): 224.

3. The name "Aristobulus" has been restored in a fragment of one of the *Mishmarot* scrolls on the basis of the first two letters. If correct, this might be Aristobulus II, the brother of Hyrcanus II (67–63 B.C.). All of the names appear on fragments without any larger context.

4. The quotations from Josephus are taken from the edition of William Whiston, with occasional necessary corrections.

5. Todd S. Beall, *Josephus' Description of the Essenes Illustrated by the Dead Sea Scrolls.* Society for New Testament Studies Monograph 58 (Cambridge: Cambridge University Press, 1988).

6. According to John Trever, Ibrahim Sowmy, the brother of one of the St. Mark's monks, theorized "that a group of Essenes owned the scrolls and hid them"—and this before any scroll had been read or even identified! (Trever, *Untold Story,* 185, n. 12).

7. His first book on the subject was *Aperçus préliminaires sur les manuscrits de la mer Morte* (1950; English translation *The Dead Sea Scrolls: A Preliminary Survey,* 1952). His definitive statement is found in *Les Écrits esséniens découverts près de la mer Morte* (1959; English translation *The Essene Writings from Qumran,* 1962).

8. See Vermes, *The Dead Sea Scrolls,* 151; Gert Jeremias, *Der Lehrer der Gerechtigkeit* (The Teacher of Righteousness) (Gottingen: Vandenhoeck & Ruprecht, 1963), 71–78; Milik, *Ten Years of Discovery in the Wilderness of Judaea,* 72.

9. Cross, *Ancient Library of Qumran,* 127–60.

10. See William H. Brownlee, "The Wicked Priest, the Man of Lies, and the Righteous Teacher—The Problem of Identity," *Jewish Quarterly Review* 73 (1982): 1–37.

11. Jerome Murphy-O'Connor, "The Essenes in Palestine," *Biblical Archaeologist* 40/3 (September 1977): 100–24; "The Essenes and Their History," *Revue Biblique* 81 (1974): 215–44.

12. The Cave 4 Nabatean documents include a letter (4Q343) and a fragment of the biblical book of Kings in Nabatean script (4Q235).

13. De Vaux's own book on the subject, *Archaeology and the Dead Sea Scrolls,* the Schweich Lectures of the British Academy, 1959 (London: Oxford University Press, 1973) is quite readable. Another introduction for nonspecialists is Philip R. Davies's *Qumran,* Cities of the Biblical World (Guildford, Surrey: Lutterworth, 1982).

14. One feature absent from the Qumran ruins is living quarters. Assuming that Khirbet Qumran was a community center of the Essenes, we must imagine them living in tents or caves in the vicinity and only coming to the buildings for work, meals, study, or meetings. The discovery of pottery and other utensils in the surrounding caves (including caves without scrolls in them) supports this idea.

15. De Vaux, *Archaeology and the Dead Sea Scrolls,* 41.

16. Davies, *Qumran,* 46.

17. Cross, "The Early History of the Qumran Community," in David Freedman and Jonas Greenfield, eds., *New Directions in Biblical Archaeology* (Garden City, N.Y.: Doubleday, 1971), 77.

18. Millar Burrows, *More Light on the Dead Sea Scrolls,* 263.

19. Jerome Murphy-O'Connor, "The Judean Desert," in R. A. Kraft and G. W. E. Nickelsburg, eds., *Early Judaism and Its Modern Interpreters* (Philadelphia: Fortress, 1986), 124.

20. An early critique of the Essene hypothesis is Cecil Roth, "Why the Qumran Sect Cannot Have Been Essenes," *Revue de Qumran* 1 (1958): 417–22.

21. A. Marx canvasses the suggestions in "Racines du Célibat Essénien" (Roots of Essene Celibacy), *Revue de Qumran* 7/27 (1970): 334–35.

22. Burrows, *The Dead Sea Scrolls,* 294. Other representatives of the "almost Essene" approach are James Sanders, who published the Cave 11 scroll of Psalms, and Shemaryahu Talmon, an Israeli scholar who serves on the Oversight Committee appointed by Amir Drori. The late William Sanford LaSor, one of the few evangelical Qumran scholars, always resisted an identification of the Qumran sect with the Essenes.

23. Cross, *Ancient Library of Qumran,* 57.

Chapter 6

Who Wrote the Scrolls? (II)

A small but vociferous group of scholars totally rejects any connection of the Dead Sea Scrolls to the Essenes. They are not particularly impressed by the parallels between the scrolls and the ancient reports of the Essenes. A number of them find fault with the archaeological and paleographical methods that de Vaux, Cross, and others developed to date the scrolls. If the fairly narrow time range defined by the occupation of Khirbet Qumran could be enlarged, then so could the possibilities for finding other groups that could have written the scrolls.

Besides the Essenes, Josephus mentions two other major Jewish sects: the Pharisees and the Sadducees. He also describes a group called the Zealots, which in his view hardly differ from the Pharisees, except in the fervor of their hatred of Roman rule. All three of these groups have been suggested as the true authors of the Dead Sea Scrolls.

The Pharisees

According to Josephus, the Pharisees were the dominant religious party in Judaism in the first century A.D. That will come as no surprise to those familiar with the New Testament. The Pharisees figure prominently in the Gospels, engaging in heated disputes with Jesus and his disciples about the Jewish law. An example is found in Mark 7:5, where the Pharisees ask Jesus, "Why don't your disciples live according to the tradition of the elders instead of eating their food with 'unclean' hands?" The conditions of ceremonial "cleanness" and "uncleanness" were a preoccupation of the Pharisees.

Josephus also mentions the "tradition of the elders," explaining that "the Pharisees have delivered to the people a great many observances by succession from their fathers, which are not written in the laws of Moses" (*Antiquities* XIII.x.6). The Pharisaic tradition, or oral law, elaborated on some of the laws of the Old Testament, as well as adding precepts on ceremonial and ethical matters not provided for in the Old Testament.

The Pharisaic tradition had a decisive role in shaping later Judaism. Rabbinic Judaism, which developed after the destruction of Jerusalem in A.D. 70, is both the heir of Pharisaism and the matrix out of which modern Judaism came. It is therefore doubly unfortunate that we know relatively little about the origins, organization, and growth of the Pharisees. We know from Josephus and the New Testament that the Pharisees were popular with the people, had an unwritten tradition, believed in the resurrection of the dead, and were meticulous about ceremonial cleanness and tithing. Later Jewish writings, looking back on the Pharisees from a distance of at least one or two centuries, relate that the Pharisees were organized into groups called *havurot* (singular *havura*). A full member of a *havura* had to promise to maintain strict ceremonial cleanness at all times. Entrance into the group proceeded by stages, as in the *Manual of Discipline*.

The statutes of the Qumran sect also resemble the Pharisaic laws. The *Damascus Document* contains a long section of laws for the Sabbath and other religious regulations, which, in many respects, tallies with Jewish law as it is found in the later compilations of rabbinic Judaism. For these reasons it has been suggested that the Qumran sect were Pharisees.[1]

It is interesting and significant that the Pharisees and sectarians have some precepts in common. It may point to a shared origin, or to some kind of mutual influence. But the differences are too many to allow any closer identification. There is no evidence that the Pharisees held goods in common, observed holidays according to a solar calendar, had a controlling hierarchy of overseers, or owed their existence to a Teacher of Righteousness. And, although many of the laws of the sect agreed with those of the Pharisees, some didn't. The law forbidding polygamy is one example. The Pharisees allowed polygamy, as did the Sadducees. The "Pharisee hypothesis" accordingly has few followers.

The Zealots

The Zealot hypothesis is a more significant challenge to the reigning Essene theory. Again, Josephus is the main source of information about the Zealots. He writes that one Judas of Galilee, around the beginning of the first century A.D., added a "fourth sect of Jewish philosophy" to the Pharisees, Sadducees, and Essenes. Josephus says in *Antiquities* that the "fourth sect" agreed in most things with the Pharisees (XVIII.i.6), and in *The Jewish War* that these "Zealots" are not at all like the rest of the sects (II.viii.1). He gives no further details about any distinctive beliefs of the Zealots other than that they believe "God to be their only Ruler and Lord" (*Antiquities* XVIII.i.6).

Scholars have been able to piece together a picture of the Zealots from Jewish tradition and Josephus' histories.[2] Today they would undoubtedly be labelled extremists, fanatics, or terrorists (to the sympathetic, "freedom fighters"). They believed in waging an uncompromising holy war against Roman occupation of Israel. Judas the Galilean taught that only God could rule Israel, making Roman rule intolerable, especially since the Roman emperors considered themselves to be divine and accepted worship as such. They believed that to pay taxes to Rome was a sin and believed that the kingdom of God—the time when God himself would redeem Israel from bondage and rule his people directly—would only come when all Jews radically separated themselves from contact with Gentiles. Obviously, marriage to Gentiles was forbidden, as was any compromise with idolatry.

The Zealots sometimes carried out their agenda by assassination or open warfare. They murdered collaborationist priests and sometimes killed non-Jews who ventured into strongly Jewish areas.

They may have forced Gentiles who worshiped the Jewish God to choose between circumcision and death. Some Zealot groups went into the Judean wilderness, living like outlaws in caves, far from the polluting presence of Gentiles.

Many other Jews longed for an end to Roman rule and the coming of God's kingdom and hated the tax collectors and the Gentile presence in the holy places of Jerusalem. The Zealots differed mainly, it seems, in the intensity of their hatred of Gentiles and in their readiness to kill and be killed for the kingdom of God, as they understood it.

The Zealots finally succeeded in raising a nationwide revolt in A.D. 66. The results were disastrous for Judea: The Romans systematically suppressed the rebellion and destroyed Jerusalem and the temple in A.D. 70. The last band of Zealots held out at the wilderness fortress of Masada until A.D. 73, committing mass suicide (according to Josephus) when the Romans were on the point of victory.

Some scholars believe the Zealots or a Zealot group wrote the Dead Sea Scrolls. They point to the hatred expressed in some of the scrolls for Gentiles or "outsider" Jews. The scrolls' obsessive concern with the purity of nation and temple reminds one of the "zeal" of the extremists. The martial fervor of the *War Scroll,* which lays down rules for the final battle against the "Sons of Darkness," fits well with what we know about the Zealots.

Furthermore, there is the intriguing fact that the Qumran settlement came to a violent end. The end of Period II—dated by de Vaux to A.D. 68—is registered by a layer of ash: Khirbet Qumran's end was fiery. The archaeologists also found arrowheads in this layer, indicating a pitched battle. Could the peace-loving, communal, monastic Essenes have posed any kind of threat to Roman rule? Or is it more logical to suppose that Roman troops were attacking a Zealot outpost?

Zealot theorists also point to the fact that scroll fragments containing parts of the Qumran *Songs for the Sabbath Sacrifice* were also found at Masada. If the *Songs* were used in sectarian worship, then it seems that the sect was a Zealot group, like their comrades at Masada. Finally, Zealot theorists have been quick to point out the shortcomings of the Essene, Pharisee, and Sadducee hypotheses. If they were not one of these three groups, the Qumran sect must have belonged to the "fourth philosophy."

J. T. Milik of the international scroll team accepted that the sect, at least towards the end, became infected with Zealotism. He called the fourth phase of the Qumran group—corresponding to Period II of the settlement—"Essenism with Zealot tendencies."

> The exiles [of Period II], especially the younger recruits, were as much filled with anti-Roman sentiments as with religious fervour. . . . At this time the *Rule of the War* was written. . . . The Zealot character of the Essene community in its last phase also explains why Qumran was destroyed by the [Roman] Legio X Fretensis in the summer of 68. It had become a centre of military resistance, or at least a school of propagandists.[3]

But most scholars felt that the Zealot hypothesis is rather weak. It is true that some Zealots lived in the Judean wilderness and hated outsiders, but there is no evidence that they formed a tight monastic group, held all goods in common, developed a dualistic worldview contrasting light and darkness, observed a solar calendar, or worked up a comprehensive set of religious laws at variance with the rest of Judaism. Most of what the scrolls and Qumran hold in common—the sole worship of God, a hatred of idolatry, the expectation of God's kingdom, and the rejection of Gentile influences—is also common to the other Jewish groups, and indeed to any group that takes the Old Testament seriously. As for the end of the settlement, who is to say that the Romans attacked only active rebels? Surely they were capable of exterminating any concentration of Jews, no matter how innocuous. And the *Songs for the Sabbath Sacrifice* were not sectarian hymns at all, but contain sentiments that could have been shared by most Jews of that period.

The Roth-Driver Theory

Two scholars holding to the Zealot identification, Cecil Roth and G. R. Driver, sought to overcome the overall weaknesses of the Zealot theory by pinning their arguments to particular interpretations of the historical hints contained in the *Habakkuk Pesher*.[4]

According to Josephus, after the Jewish revolt broke out in A.D. 66, a Zealot leader named Menahem marched up to Jerusalem with his followers. There he arrayed himself in royal garments and set himself up as the leader of the revolt. The rebel leaders already in Jerusalem, led by the captain of the temple, Eleazar, resented Menahem's attempt to highjack the revolution and plotted to kill him. When Menahem and his bodyguard went to the temple to worship, Eleazar's followers attacked them and pursued Menahem to the hill of Ophel south of the temple. There he was captured, tortured, and killed, along with another Zealot chieftain named Absalom. The rest of Menahem's followers fled to the fortress of Masada in the wilderness of Judea.

Roth and Driver claimed that this incident is narrated in a mysterious passage of the *Habbakuk Pesher* in which each verse of the prophecy is made to reflect some event of the writer's times or the sect's history. The passage in question is:

> The Wicked Priest pursued the Teacher of Righteousness to destroy him in his hot anger in the place of his exile; and in the time appointed for the repose of the Day of Atonement, he appeared to them to destroy them and to overthrow them on the fast day of their Sabbath rest (XI, 4–8).

According to Roth and Driver, the Teacher of Righteousness was Menahem, the Wicked Priest Eleazar. The scroll later even mentions the "House of Absalom," the name of Menahem's compatriot. They argued that this event took place on or near the Day of Atonement, as specified in the *Pesher*.

But there is no evidence that Menahem was a sectarian religious teacher, like the Teacher, or that his assassination took place on the Day of Atonement or that Eleazar was a priest. Nothing the scrolls say about the Teacher indicates that he was a military leader. The *Habakkuk Pesher* rebukes the "House of Absalom" because they "were silent at the rebuke of the Teacher of Righteousness and did not help him against the Man of the Lie" (V, 10–11). This does not sound much like the Absalom who died at Menahem's side. Nor, finally, does the *Pesher* state that the Teacher was killed, although that apparently was the Priest's intention. As de Vaux said, "There is no need to be astonished at 'coincidences' which do not exist."[5]

The Zealot theory in this form therefore failed to win much support. But Roth and Driver did succeed in laying the groundwork for a more sustained critique of the Essene hypothesis, pointing out some weaknesses in the arguments from paleography and archaeology used by the "establishment" scholars.

For the Zealot theory to work, most of de Vaux's archaeological conclusions had to be ignored. Menahem died in A.D. 66. If he was the founder of the sect, then the literature of the sect—the Dead Sea Scrolls—had to have been written in the first and possibly second centuries A.D. and not in the first and second centuries B.C. How can this be squared with the evidence of pottery, paleography, carbon-14 tests, and historical references? What about the evidence linking Khirbet Qumran and the scrolls—for instance, the scriptorium? What about the evidence that the settlement was destroyed in A.D. 68?

Roth and Driver—and in this, at least, they were not alone—were not convinced. They denied (lamely) the force of the coin evidence,[6] but argued, with more reason, against the paleographical method. Driver pointed out that although paleographers may place the development of letters in a sequence (as we did with *samek*), the sequence does not necessarily imply a chronology. Although "closed" *samek* comes after "open" *samek*, it is possible, even likely, that old conservative scribes kept on writing open *samek* while their daring young proteges wrote it closed. But scrolls written by both types of scribes in the same month might look as if they should be separated by a generation. Hence the idea that a copy of a particular scroll can be dated to a twenty-five-year period is absurd.

As for the scriptorium, Driver pointed out that the "tables" found at Qumran were not necessarily writing tables; in fact, there is no evidence that scribes wrote on tables in this period. If there was no scriptorium at Qumran, a major link between the scrolls and the settlement is broken.

Roth and Driver also claimed that there is no reason to connect the end of the Qumran settlement with the deposit of the scrolls. Even if some of the scrolls were written there, and if the settlement did end in A.D. 68, who is to say that the sect had to get rid of all their scrolls when their buildings were burned down? Why couldn't they just move somewhere else? Surely not all of them were killed. Are we to suppose that they all gave up Essenism (or whatever), dumped their scrolls in the caves, and faded away? If they survived, they probably kept writing scrolls; if they kept writing scrolls, then some of the Dead Sea Scrolls might be from a time after A.D. 68. If they are, then the Zealot theory is theoretically possible. So is any other theory that requires a date later in the first century A.D.

These weaknesses in the paleographical and archaeological evidence still do not add up to a complete counter-theory. A real counter-theory has to prove itself on the basis of the written evidence, and the Zealot theory has not. And even the weaknesses in the nonwritten evidence can be overblown. It is true that unjustifiable precision has been claimed for paleography, but it is still useful for setting broad chronological limits. Although the great Isaiah scroll from Cave 1 cannot be dated to the year or the decade, no responsible scholar would claim that it was later than the first century B.C. As for the archaeology, the caves also contained pottery that is remarkably similar to that found in Khirbet Qumran, but little pottery from a period later than the ruin. This implies that the caves were used at the same time as the Qumran buildings but no later. Finally, the scrolls themselves contain unmistakable references to events of the second and first centuries B.C. There are no comparable references to the first century A.D. In the end, if the Essene theory is shaky, the Zealot theory in this form is shakier.

Nevertheless, de Vaux's inferences from the Qumran excavation are now being reevaluated. Like many archaeologists, he never published in full the results of the excavation. Many now believe that de Vaux's conclusions should be treated with reserve until all the objects from the excavation—some of which have been misplaced or lost since de Vaux's death—are reexamined. Belgian scholar Robert Donceel has been given the task of putting de Vaux's excavation report in order.

Where does this leave us? With a number of more or less shaky theories, it seems. Readers at this point may ruefully feel that the Qumran sect disappeared simply for being so endlessly incomprehensible; or they may feel sympathy with Hyman's remark about a "Sunday outing on the madhouse lawn." The only way to break the impasse is with new evidence, that is, with new texts. It is indeed the publication of some new texts that have given new life to yet another theory: that the sectarians were Sadducees.

The Saduccees—or the Zadokites?

"What!" said the Colonel. "Do you mean to tell me you don't believe in second-sight, or ghosts, or anything of that kind?"

> "In nothing whatever of that kind," returned Parkins firmly.
>
> "Well," said the Colonel, "but it appears to me at that rate, sir, that you must be little better than a Sadducee."
>
> Parkins was on the point of answering that, in his opinion, the Sadducees were the most sensible persons he had ever read of in the Old Testament; but, feeling some doubt as to whether much mention of them was to be found in that work, he preferred to laugh the accusation off.[7]

The average Bible reader might feel as much doubt as the fictional Professor Parkins about who exactly the Sadducees were and what they believed. They are mentioned in the New Testament, of course, not the Old; but the Gospels, Acts, and that usually dependable fount of information, Josephus, tell us comparatively little about them.

Both the New Testament and Josephus agree that the Sadducees did not believe in life after death or the resurrection of the dead. "The Sadducees say that there is no resurrection, and that there are neither angels nor spirits, but the Pharisees acknowledge them all" (Acts 23:8). Both sources also agree that the Jerusalem priests were Sadducees (Acts 5:17). Josephus observes that the Sadducees, unlike the Pharisees and Essenes, believe that "to act what is good, or what is evil, is at men's own choice, and that the one or the other belongs so to every one, that they may act as they please" (*Jewish War* II.viii.14). And later Christian authors report that the Sadducees regarded only the Pentateuch, the five books of Moses, as binding Scripture.

Even from this scanty information, it is hard to see how the Qumran sect could have been Sadducees. The sect clearly believed in "angels and spirits"; the *War Scroll* explicitly says that the "angels of holiness are with their host" (VII,6); the *Rule of the Congregation* says that "the angels of holiness are in their congregation" (II,8), and the *Manual of Discipline* speaks of the "Angel of Darkness," the "Angel of Truth," and the "Angels of Destruction." The Sadducean belief in human freewill is contrary to the Qumranian doctrine of predestination; and the apparent Sadducean neglect of the Old Testament prophets cannot be squared with the commentaries on the prophets found among the Dead Sea Scrolls.

Despite these problems, the "Sadducean hypothesis" has always had its advocates. In fact, variations of this hypothesis have lately been gaining ground on the Essene theory. There are a number of reasons for this.

First, there are some passages in the Dead Sea Scrolls that refer to the leaders of the sect as the "sons of Zadok." The *Damascus Document* says that "the 'sons of Zadok' are the chosen of Israel, those called by name, who appear in the latter days" (IV,4–5); in the *Manual of Discipline,* the new initiates pledge to obey the sons of Zadok (V,2), and so on. Thus, to be called a Zadokite was a claim to priestly legitimacy.

Zadok is the Old Testament figure who was high priest under David and Solomon. According to the book of Ezekiel, the descendants of Zadok "are the only Levites who may draw near to the LORD to minister before him" (Ezek. 40:46). The word *Sadducees* (Greek: *Saddoukaioi*) is apparently derived from this proper name Zadok: "Sadducee" means "Zadokite." So a link between the Sadducees and the Qumranian "Zadokites" exists in their common use of this proper name. Both the Sadducees and the Qumran sect were led by priests who claimed the name of Zadok.

The scholars who have developed a hypothesis of Zadokite/Sadducean origins for the Dead Sea Scrolls admit that the Qumran Zadokites cannot be identical to the Sadducees mentioned by Josephus and the New Testament,[8] but argue that they were a group that split off from the "establishment" Sadducees for a number of reasons. The Sadducean love of wealth might have been one reason. The *Damascus Document* denounces "the filthy lucre of wickedness gotten by vow or by consecration or by Temple wealth" (VI,15–16). This could well refer to the establishment Sadducees. For whatever reason, the Qumran group turned its back on the temple and the Jerusalem priesthood and became "dropout" Sadducees. We have already noted how prominent priests were in the Qumran sect. Perhaps the whole group was of priestly origin.

Recent developments and discoveries have caused Qumran scholars to take another look at the Sadducee theory, which never won many adherents in the early days of scroll research. Two new documents, the *Temple Scroll* and especially the writing known as *Miksat Ma'asei ha-Torah* (Some Deeds of the Law, usually referred to as 4QMMT)—have forced a reevaluation of this hypothesis.

The *Temple Scroll,* although primarily a rewriting, harmonization, and expansion of the Mosaic legislation found in Exodus,

Leviticus, and Deuteronomy, also contains precepts not derived from the Old Testament. 4QMMT is a treatise discussing twenty points of Jewish law in which one group, speaking in the first person, describes its differences from a group it is addressing ("we think . . . although you say"). Strugnell and Qimron first described it as a "letter" written from the Teacher of Righteousness to his opponents.

One example of agreement between the *Temple Scroll,* 4QMMT, and Sadducean practice will be treated here at some length. Many readers may find the discussion of a fine point of Jewish law tedious. But for Judaism, variations in such practices were of far greater importance than variations in seemingly larger theological questions. Differences on a number of practical questions might well lead to a schism, whereas differing opinions on, say, "fate" probably would not. So the issue of religious law is crucial.

Numbers 19:1–10 gives the details of the ceremony of the red heifer. The red heifer was to be slaughtered and burned outside the camp of the Israelites and its ashes gathered up and kept in a ceremonially clean place for use in the "waters of cleansing." This holy water was important because it was the only means by which certain kinds of uncleanness could be removed; an unclean person could not worship in the temple or touch anyone or anything that was clean.

According to rabbinic literature, the Sadducees and Pharisees differed over the degree of ritual cleanness necessary for the high priest who was to slaughter the red heifer. Numbers 19 specifies that those who slaughter and burn the heifer and gather its ashes must then immerse themselves and wait until sunset before they are completely clean again. The Sadducees said that they also had to immerse themselves and wait until sunset *before* the ritual to be in a proper state of cleanness. The Pharisees agreed that the high priest should immerse himself but that he did not have to wait until sunset. So insistent were the Pharisees on this point that they would deliberately defile the high priest on his way to perform the ritual. That way he would have time only to immerse himself before the slaughter took place, but not to wait for sunset:

> In the case of the Red Heifer we defile the high priest, for we learnt, they used to defile the priest who was to burn the heifer and then

> make him immerse, in order to combat the opinion of the Sadducees, who maintained: the ceremony was to be performed only by those on whom the sun had set.[9]

Now the *Temple Scroll* contains no precepts about the red heifer ritual, but it does insist that, in general, complete ritual cleanness is available only for those who have both immersed themselves and waited until sundown (45:7–8; 49:19–21; 51:4–5). That implies a certain connection to the Sadducees. But an explicit connection is found in 4QMMT, which also says that sundown was necessary to "complete" the ritual cleansing for the personnel involved in the red heifer ritual:

> Concerning the purity of the "heifer of expiation," the one who slaughters it and the one who burns it and the one who gathers its ashes and the one who sprinkles the blood of the sacrifice—all of these must wait until sundown [before the sacrifice] to be clean, in order that the clean should purify the unclean (B 13–15).

This text seems to provide a clear link to the Sadducees.

Another link is the 4QMMT law concerning the unbroken stream of liquid. The Pharisees held that if you poured a clear liquid from a vessel that was ceremonially clean into one that was unclean, the uncleanness did not travel up the stream to "infect" the clean vessel. The Sadducees, however, believed that the uncleanness of the receiving vessel was contagious through the stream of liquid.[10] So did the Qumran sect:

> Concerning the poured out liquids we say that there is no cleanness in them, and moreover the poured out liquids do not divide unclean from clean, because the moisture of the poured out liquids and the vessel that receives them are alike one moisture (4QMMT B 55–58).

Although these differences in religious law may seem to be sheer nitpicking, they were highly significant. Pharisees, Sadducees, and Essenes were very careful to avoid becoming ritually unclean. If differences existed about who was clean and who was not, they could lead to drastic separation between the sects. The Sadducees may well have believed that the Pharisees were always unclean; we know that the Pharisees (whose name means "the separated") felt the same about the majority of laypeople who were not interested in purity laws. Disputes centering on purity formed a significant portion of the Pharisees' disputes with Jesus and his disciples (see Mark 7).

The similarity between the religious law of the *Temple Scroll,* 4QMMT, and the Sadducees requires some sort of connection between the Sadducees and the Dead Sea Scrolls. Lawrence Schiffman, one of the advocates of the Sadducean approach, says:

> MMT revolutionizes the question of Qumran origins and requires us to reconsider the entire Essene hypothesis. It shows beyond question that either the sect was not Essene, but was Sadducean, or that the Essene movement must be totally redefined as having emerged out of Sadducean beginnings.

Schiffman believes that "a group of originally Sadducean priests, under the leadership of the Teacher of Righteousness . . . developed into the group that left us the sectarian texts found at Qumran."[11]

Not everybody agrees that the question of Qumran origins has been "revolutionized" by 4QMMT. James Vanderkam of Notre Dame claims that the Sadducee hypothesis is "most improbable," due to the importance of the Essene traits, which cannot be explained away. Neither can the Sadducean doctrines about angels, fate, and so on.[12] But it should be noted that the Sadducean theory is not necessarily incompatible with the Essene hypothesis. For all we know, "drop-out" Sadducees were called "Essenes":

> The Sadducees were not a monolithic sect. They also had divisions and arduous struggles. The extremists among them—those with pronounced religious, ethical, and spiritual leanings—that is, the Essenes—disgusted with the petrified priestly cult and with the behavior of the aristocratic priests, were forced to divide both from the temple and from the mass of people.[13]

Some such compromise solution—that the Essenes were "break-away" Sadducees—seems likely to be the preferred option for a while in Qumran studies, at least until some newly published text stirs things up again.

The Jerusalem Hypothesis of Norman Golb

Who wrote the Dead Sea Scrolls? The preceding discussion shows how hard it is to fit all the texts and other evidence together to give a consistent answer. One scholar, Norman Golb of the

University of Chicago, has come up with a highly original alternative: The Dead Sea Scrolls are not the library of any particular group, but a collection of libraries from a number of groups, forming a cross section of all Jewish literature from the period around the first century A.D.

At first glance, this explanation seems to satisfy many problems surrounding the scrolls. If the *War Scroll* sounds like a Zealot writing, perhaps that is because it is one. If 4QMMT sounds like the Sadducees, then let it be a Sadducean writing. Does the *Manual of Discipline* read like an Essene document? Then it was written by Essenes. According to Golb, the scrolls come from every type of Judaism, not just one sectarian group.

> Without special pleading or forced exegesis, all current evidence leads to the conclusion that the scrolls originated in Jerusalem and were taken to hiding places in the Judean wilderness for safekeeping either before or during the Roman siege on Jerusalem of A.D. 70.[14]

That is, the Dead Sea Scrolls were left by inhabitants of Jerusalem fleeing the advancing Roman army during the revolt of A.D. 66–70.[15]

To achieve this gratifying simplicity, Golb focuses on four main problems. One is the weakness of the Essene hypothesis, based on the discrepancies already mentioned. The second is the dubious link between the scrolls and Khirbet Qumran. The third is the anomaly of the *Copper Scroll*. The fourth is the incompatibility of the scrolls with each other.

Golb attacks the link between the scrolls and Qumran by noting that ancient sources mention other manuscript cave finds near Jericho, providing an alternate pattern for the scroll deposits. If the ancient inhabitants of Jericho hid their scrolls for safekeeping, then maybe the ancient inhabitants of Jerusalem did the same thing. A scroll-writing outpost in the wilderness is not required. Golb further argues, with Roth and Driver, that Khirbet Qumran was probably a fortress, not an Essene "monastery."

Even more important for Golb is the nature of the *Copper Scroll*. "Mainstream" theorists debated whether that list of buried treasure was authentic or fantastic. Whether the scroll is real or fictional, it is hard to see the mysterious document as part and parcel of the rest of the manuscript cache. It was written in a different dialect of Hebrew from the rest, on different material, and deals with totally different subjects. De Vaux himself was forced to conclude that the *Copper Scroll* had to be considered as a unique Dead Sea Scroll that should be studied apart from the other manuscripts:

> It would be easier to explain the unique character of this document, so foreign to the outlook and preoccupations of the community, if it emanated from some other source and had been deposited at a later stage.[16]

(Milik dated it paleographically at around A.D. 100.)

Golb believes the *Copper Scroll* is authentic and that the place names and different treasures the scroll mentions clearly point to a Jerusalem origin: "The palpable place of origin of the treasures, artifacts, and books referred to . . . is Jerusalem." The treasure of the *Copper Scroll* is composed of "the sizable treasures that had accumulated in the Temple."[17] This could not be the treasure of the poverty-loving communal Essenes. And if that scroll can be seen as somehow a contamination of the sectarian library from another time and place, then this breaks up the distinctiveness necessary for identifying the scrolls as the product of a single group. Indeed, Golb does not see any unity at all in the scrolls, finding so many contradictions in law and theology between them that they cannot be the product of a single sect.

Golb considers these and other arguments so convincing that he has to accuse other scholars of self-interested blindness:

> Scholars in general are no different than other men and women in being loath to change their ideas, particularly if they have garnered fame or recognition for having expressed them. They are equally loath to see those ideas challenged.[18]

Golb may be right about the entrenchment of certain ideas in the scholarly mind. People get attached to ideas, especially their own, and the borders between acceptable and unacceptable theories are often drawn more by fashion or prejudice than by impartial scrutiny of the evidence.

Nevertheless, it appears that Golb's "Jerusalem hypothesis" has failed to gain supporters because it is based on weak arguments. The connection of the scrolls to the ruin is one example. This connection is not airtight, nor has anyone ever claimed that it is more than probable. Still, Golb's theories are not a viable alternative. De Vaux already pointed out that the presence at Qumran of the ancient cemetery of over a thousand graves is not the sort of thing one would find next to a fortress.[19] Golb also makes much of the graves of women found in the cemetery as refuting the celibate-Essene theory. Perhaps—but they also mean that Khirbet Qumran could hardly have been a military outpost. Golb is aware that the pottery of the caves and the ruin are very similar, but lamely says that "the inhabitants of the region"—including the "fortress"?—furnished the fleeing refugees with jars for their scrolls![20] As for the ancient manuscript find at Jericho, we do not know what those texts were or who hid them or when or where or why. Some believe the ancient reports refer to an earlier ransacking of the Qumran caves.

But Golb has identified a real problem with the *Copper Scroll*, which remains the "most mysterious of all the Dead Sea Scrolls," in John Allegro's words. (It is now being restudied by Prof. P. Kyle McCarter of the Johns Hopkins University.) And Golb has succeeded in raising the consciousness of many about the diversity of texts from Qumran. Partly because of his criticisms, scholars are much more careful than they used to be about calling a particular work "sectarian" and assigning its composition to the Qumran sect.

Nevertheless, Golb has overemphasized the diversity of the sectarian scrolls and understated their unity. There are difficulties in understanding how all the scrolls fit into one religious system, but the common elements in the scrolls are so pervasive that it is difficult to see them as totally separated in origin. Are we really supposed to think that several different sects in Jerusalem called their leader the Teacher of Righteousness, or that every group writing in Jerusalem unaccountably kept a heterodox solar calendar, or that the entire populace had a keen interest in the *Book of Jubilees* (fifteen copies from Cave 4) and almost none in Proverbs (two) or Chronicles (one small fragment)?

Many Qumran scholars have suggested that the group (whoever they were) underwent certain changes in outlook as they evolved, and that their literature (like the *Damascus Document* and the *Manual of Discipline*) was successively revised or recombined with other works as these changes took place. Scholars have identified different versions of both of these works from Cave 4 that support the idea that they and other Qumran texts went through several "revised editions." Golb has hurt his cause by remaining aloof from other research. He has not analyzed any text in detail or discussed serious and sophisticated theories of the sect's history. The result is that he still stands alone in his "Jerusalem hypothesis."

Solving the Mysteries: Where Are We Now?

The theories I have outlined have been in place since the early sixties. Only the Sadducee theory has received substantial new life since that time, due to the availability of 4QMMT. But since November 1991, scholars have had more or less unlimited access to all the hitherto unpublished Dead Sea Scrolls. There is now a wealth of new information. Does any of it bear on the question, "Who wrote the scrolls?"

The unsatisfying answer is "probably." There are no more texts that mention the Teacher of Righteousness, the Wicked Priest, or the Teacher's internal opponent, the Man of the Lie. Apparently no more direct information will be coming out about those figures from the Cave 4 texts. None of the "new scrolls" contain any "smoking-gun" type of information pointing to Essenes, Sadducees, Pharisees, Zealots, or other groups. And it will take scholars a long time to sift through all the material, translate it accurately, and fit it into what is known already from the published texts.

A Zealot Text?

Some texts, however, have already been canvassed for what they can tell us about the sect's origin. Robert Eisenman and Michael Wise in particular, are proponents of a "neo-Zealot" theory of the Dead Sea Scrolls. In their recent book, *The Dead Sea Scrolls Uncovered,* they publish a text (4Q471) they call "The Servants of Darkness." Their comment is, "The violence, xenophobia, passionate nationalism, and concern for Righteousness and the Judgments of God are evident throughout. . . . It is impossible to think that those writing these texts were not steeped in the ethos of a militant army of God."[21] In their translation, the relevant portion of the fragmentary text reads:

> . . . the time You have commanded them not to . . . and you shall lie about His Covenant . . . they say, Let us fight His wars, for we have polluted . . . your [enemies] shall be brought low, and they shall not

> know that by fire . . . gather courage for war, and you shall be reckoned . . . you shall ask of the experts of Righteous Judgment and the service of . . . you shall be lifted up, for He chose [you] . . . for shouting . . . and you shall bur[n . . .] and sweet

Taken at face value, this obscure text certainly seems to breathe a militant air that matches up with what we know of the Zealots. And yet Eisenman and Wise have not necessarily interpreted and translated the text rightly. Two Israeli scholars, Esther Eshel and Menahem Kister, have recently discussed the same text and come to a reading diametrically opposed to Eisenman and Wise's. Their translation:

> . . . you were commanded not to . . . and you violated His covenant . . . you said, "We shall fight his battles, because He redeemed us" . . . your [ ] will be brought low, and they did not know that He despised[22] . . . you become mighty[23] for battle, and you were accounted[24] . . . ??[25] You seek righteous judgement and service of . . . you are arrogant. And he chose [them?] . . . to the cry . . . and You will put . . . sweet[26]

If Eshel and Kister have understood the fragment more accurately, 4Q471 is a text *opposing* those who feel that they are fighting God's battles. The opponents could be Zealots. If the text is considered to be earlier than the first century A.D., as seems likely, then the opponents could be the militant Hasmonean priest-kings. After the Maccabees won religious freedom from the Greeks in the second century B.C., the Hasmonean leaders embarked on a long series of wars designed to secure political freedom and to expand the borders of Judea. Eshel and Kister believe that 4Q471 is directed against the Hasmoneans, who had "been false to His covenant" by rejecting the sect's interpretation of the Torah. Because of the Maccabean military successes, they believed they were fighting God's battles. Yet they were unaware that God had rejected them. Although the Hasmonean rulers vaunted themselves for battle, they were not accounted as righteous; instead, they were arrogant.

Nor could a Zealot much like the sentiments of the still untitled scroll 4Q460. Fragmentary as it is, its slant on war is clear:

> Let not warriors boast themselves [in their strength . . .] in their might, nor kings in the power of their strength, nor princes [. . .] in their weapons of war or in their strong cities [. . . Our God, there is

> none] like Him, there is none more glorious [. . .] glorious to help us, and a [fortified] wall . . .[27]

The writer praises God as helper, not earthly weapons of war.

Other New Texts

The Essene hypothesis does not gain any more support from the new scrolls either. Indeed, if celibacy is considered to be a benchmark of true Essenism, then the new texts simply add to the evidence that the Qumran sect allowed marriage. The text 4Q251 goes into some detail about who a man is *not* allowed to marry—which would make no sense if he were not allowed to marry at all.[28] Another text (4Q274) gives rules for the purification of menstruating women or men who have seminal emissions. Still another text—the "sapiential work" (4Q416)—speaks of "taking a wife," "joining together with the help of your flesh," "becoming one flesh," and alludes to sons and daughters.[29]

Another text should be mentioned. It is 4Q477, called "The Decrees of the Sect." The unique feature of this fragment is that it mentions particular names of sect members and describes their offenses and the corresponding penalties:

> . . . and also the men of the community . . . their soul to reprove . . . camps of the many . . . and [they reproved] John son of Matthew; he is short tempered. . . . he has the evil eye, and also a desire for adornment (?) . . . and Ananias Nitus they reproved because he . . . to trouble the spirit of the community and also to mingle (?) . . . son of Joseph because he has the evil eye and also because he is not . . . and also he loves the emission (?) of his flesh . . . and Ananias son of Simeon they reproved . . . and also he loves . . . [30]

This passage is not easily understood. But one thing is clear: that the sect enforced real discipline on real people with names. That may seem elementary. But some scholars, despairing of finding a historical niche for the sect, have taken the tack that the Dead Sea Scrolls are purely utopian schemes that some ancient scribes concocted for an ideal, but nonexistent, sect. Scroll 4Q477 refutes that theory.

One final text is worth mentioning, a group of fragments from a scroll that is now simply called "Zedekiah." It is difficult to get a coherent story from these fragments, but what is readable is interesting:

> . . . Michael . . . [he call]ed Zedekiah in that day . . . to do and to cause to do the Torah . . . in that time and Michael said to Zedekiah . . . "I shall make with [you a covenant] before the assembly . . ."[31]

This Zedekiah is probably not a biblical figure; all of the Zedekiahs of the Old Testament are either nonentities or villains. But in this text a certain Zedekiah speaks to Michael the archangel. Their conversation has something to do with keeping the Torah and causing others to keep it. Michael, elsewhere referred to in the scrolls as the "Spirit of Truth" or the "Prince of Light"—that is, the leader of the Sons of Light—makes a covenant with Zedekiah before the assembly. Who is this enigmatic Zedekiah?

The name "Zedekiah" includes the Hebrew word for "righteousness" (*zedek*). Is it possible that Zedekiah is the proper name of the Teacher of Righteousness (*moreh ha-zedek*)? If so, the Zedekiah scroll may once have contained a narrative about the "call" of the Teacher.

Conclusion

The bottom line is that the new texts widen and deepen our understanding of the sect. But at least after an initial glance, they do not radically change previous impressions of the group, nor do they aid in identifying it with any historical faction. Unless a "magic scroll" is discovered that solves all the problems, scholars are going to keep on having different opinions about the Dead Sea Scrolls. We will be lucky if a rough consensus emerges. But even that will take a long time. After almost fifty years, we are still closer to the beginning, not the end, of Dead Sea Scrolls research.

This brief summary of some currents in Qumran research can only frustrate those who seek a "unified field theory" of the Dead Sea Scrolls. The historical data are regrettably few. Although some interpretations have found greater favor than others, none have gone uncontested. The investigation will continue for years to come; but right now any claim to have solved all the mysteries of the Dead Sea Scrolls must be received with reserve. That is also the case with the theorists to be considered next, those who seek to understand the sect and its Teacher in terms of the most successful "sect" from the first century A.D.: Christianity.

Notes

1. The similarities between the Pharisaic *havura* and the Qumran community were pointed out by Saul Lieberman, "The Discipline in the So-Called Dead Sea Manual of Discipline," *Journal of Biblical Literature* 71 (1952): 199–206. Louis Ginzberg, before the discovery of the scrolls, pointed out the essentially Pharisaic nature of the *Damascus Document* regulations in *An Unknown Jewish Sect* (New York: Jewish Theological Seminary, 1970). Chaim Rabin has pressed the Pharisaic identification most strongly in his *Qumran Studies* (Oxford: Oxford University Press, 1957).

2. For what follows, I have mainly followed the excellent book by Martin Hengel, *The Zealots: Investigations into the Jewish Freedom Movement in the Period from Herod I until 70 A.D.* (Edinburgh: T & T Clark, 1989; a translation of *Die Zeloten* [Leiden: Brill, 1961]). The scholarly fashion today is to limit the term "Zealot" to only one nationalistic group that emerged at the beginning of the revolt. I have followed the older practice of referring to all violently nationalist groups as "Zealots."

3. J. T. Milik, *Ten Years of Discovery in the Wilderness of Judaea,* trans. John Strugnell. Studies in Biblical Theology 26 (Naperville, Ill.: Alec Allenson, 1959), 95–97.

4. Roth's version of the theory appeared in two books and fourteen articles dating from 1958 to 1965, Driver's in one hefty book of 624 pages, *The Judean Scrolls: A Problem and a Solution* (Oxford: Blackwell, 1965). Although Driver's theory struck at the heart of de Vaux's work, the men remained friends. Driver wrote the foreword to de Vaux's *Archaeology and the Dead Sea Scrolls,* which contained a rebuttal of his own views.

5. De Vaux, *Archaeology and the Dead Sea Scrolls,* 121.

6. Driver, *Judean Scrolls,* 394–96. Driver said that just because Jewish coins ceased at the settlement in A.D. 68, to be followed by Roman coins, does not mean that the "monastery" changed hands in A.D. 68. Since Jerusalem, the source of the coins, was under siege in 68, it is possible that the sectarians just could not get Jewish coins and had to use Roman ones. But de Vaux's point was that because the occupation levels changed precisely at the point when the coin sequence changed, it pointed to a change of ownership at the settlement. Driver tries to evade the force of this argument by asserting that the obviously Roman remains of Level III are sectarian work, since "the Jews were thoroughly familiar with Roman military structures" (396)! He follows this statement by arguing that the Romans would not have built a fortress at such an unstrategic spot as Qumran, apparently forgetting that he had just argued that the sectarians had built a fortress there.

7. M. R. James, "Oh, Whistle, and I'll Come to You, My Lad," in *Ghost Stories of an Antiquary* (1904, many republications).

8. Early pioneers of this theory were Robert North, "The Qumran 'Sadducees,'" *Catholic Biblical Quarterly* 17 (1955): 164–88, and William Sanford LaSor, *Amazing Dead Sea Scrolls and the Christian Faith* (Chicago: Moody, 1956), 195–200.

9. From the Babylonian Talmud, *Zevahim* 21a; see also the Mishnah, *Parah* 3:6–8.

10. Mishnah, *Yadayim* 4:6.

11. Lawrence Schiffman, "The Significance of the Scrolls," *Bible Review* 6/5 (October 1990): 24 (both quotes).

12. James Vanderkam, "The People of the Dead Sea Scrolls: Essenes or Sadducees?" *Bible Review* 7 (April 1991): 46.

13. Yaakov Sussman, "The History of Halakha and the Dead Sea Scrolls: Preliminary Observations on *Miksat maasei ha-torah*" (in modern Hebrew), *Tarbiz* 59 (1989–90): 69–70.

14. Norman Golb, "The Dead Sea Scrolls: A New Perspective," *American Scholar* 58 (1989): 178–79.

15. Golb's main articles on the subject are "The Problem of Origin and Identification of the Dead Sea Scrolls," *Proceedings of the American Philosoplical Society* 124 (1980): 1–24; "Who Hid the Dead Sea Scrolls?" *Biblical Archaeologist* 28 (1987): 68–82; and "The Dead Sea Scrolls: A New Perspective" (cited above). Professor Golb is now writing a book on the subject. A comprehensive discussion can be found in F. Garcia-Martinez and A. S. van der Woude, "A 'Groningen' Hypothesis of Qumran Origins and Early History," *Revue de Qumran* 14 (1990): 521–41.

16. De Vaux, *Archaeology and the Dead Sea Scrolls,* 109.

17. Golb, "Dead Sea Scrolls," 196.

18. Ibid., 206.

19. De Vaux, *Archaelogy and the Dead Sea Scrolls,* 106.

20. Golb, "Dead Sea Scrolls," 195.

21. R. Eisenman and M. Wise, *The Dead Sea Scrolls Uncovered* (Shaftesbury, U.K.: Elcment Books, 1992), 30. The translation following is from page 32.

22. Or "He rejected." Eisenman and Wise's "by fire" is based on a wholly different perception of the Hebrew letters; the text seems to be as Eshel and Kister read it.

23. Or, "you vaunt yourselves."

24. Or, "yet you were accounted. . . ." Eisenman and Wise's translation "you shall be reckoned" ignores the inflection of the Hebrew verb, which is clearly past tense.

25. The Hebrew letters here (Eisenman and Wise's "of the experts") are difficult to understand without a context; Eshel and Kister suggest that it might be read as "[as a drunken man who staggers] in his vomit."

26. Esther Eshel and Menahem Kister, "A Polemical Qumran Fragment," *Journal of Jewish Studies* 43 (1992): 278. The Hebrew text is also transliterated in Wacholder and Abegg's *Preliminary Edition of the Unpublished Dead Sea Scrolls: Fascicle Two,* 294.

27. The text is to be published in Wacholder and Abegg's third volume of transcriptions.

28. The text is found in Eisenman and Wise, *Dead Sea Scrolls Uncovered,* 200–205.

29. The Hebrew text is in Wacholder and Abegg, 2:58. The context is fragmentary.

30. The text is printed in Eisenman and Wise, *Dead Sea Scrolls Uncovered,* 272–73. My readings of the photographs differ from theirs in some respects.

31. The Hebrew text of 4Q470 ("Zedekiah") can be found in Wacholder and Abegg, 2:292.

Chapter 7

Christianity in the Dead Sea Scrolls?

The Dead Sea Scrolls would never have made it to the front pages if there were not a popular feeling that they have something to do with the origins of Christianity. As one specialist wrote, "It is as a potential threat to Christianity, its claims, and its doctrines that the scrolls have caught the imagination of laymen and clergy."[1] But the fact is that scholars are much less preoccupied than the general public (or the media) with the subject of "Christianity and the scrolls." There are two basic reasons for this: (1) the Dead Sea Scrolls contain no reference to Jesus, his teaching, crucifixion, or resurrection, the activity of his disciples, or the characteristic beliefs of the early church; and (2) most scholars believe that the majority of the Dead Sea Scrolls were written before the ministry of Christ and the rise of the early church. In short, the Dead Sea Scrolls do not and could not have a direct connection to Jesus Christ and early Christianity. This has been, and continues to be, the position of most specialists in the field.

Nevertheless, there have been a few scholars who disagree with that position. Some, like André Dupont-Sommer and John Allegro agree with the pre-Christian dating of the scrolls but believe that the early Christians borrowed most of their ideas and characteristic beliefs about Jesus from the Essene/Qumran sect. They have to argue for a "Christianity before Christ." Other scholars, such as Barbara Thiering or Robert Eisenman, say that while there are no overt references to Jesus in the scrolls, there are concealed references to him and to his disciples. They must therefore argue that the consensus dating of most scrolls in the pre-Christian period is wrong. Finally there is Jose O'Callaghan, who believes that there are New Testament texts among the Qumran fragments.

These mavericks have generally received more attention from the media than from their fellow scholars. Some of them accuse the rest of the field of narrow-minded prejudice arising from fear—fear that the New Testament will be undermined, fear that the uniqueness of Christ will be compromised, fear of the loss of church power, fear of swimming against the tide, fear of truth.

These are serious accusations to make against an entire subdiscipline of biblical studies, especially one that now contains at least as many Jews as Christians and far more liberal Protestants than conservative evangelicals. Why would the Jewish Yigael Yadin worry about undermining Christian truth? Why would liberal Protestants like Millar Burrows or Frank Moore Cross conceal the "truth" about the ministry of Christ? Why would the evangelical Martin Abegg risk his career to open up access to the unpublished scrolls if they were damaging to his faith? Of all the wild accusations thrown up by academic quarrels, the charge that Christian faith has inhibited scholarship on the scrolls is one of the silliest. Millar Burrows's statement from thirty-five years ago is still valid:

> It is quite true that as a liberal Protestant I do not share all the beliefs of my more conservative brethren. It is my considered conclusion, however, that if one will go through any of the historic statements of Christian faith he will find nothing that has been or can be disproved by the Dead Sea Scrolls. This is as true of things that I myself do not believe as it is of my most firm and cherished convictions. If I were so rash as to undertake a theological debate with a professor from either the Moody Bible Institute or Fordham University [a Catholic institution]—which God forbid—I fear I should find no ammunition in the Dead Sea Scrolls to use against them.[2]

The theory that the scrolls are directly linked to early Christianity, like any theory, has to stand or fall by an examination of the evidence. The scholars surveyed in this chapter deserve credit for raising the question. Even hypotheses that are finally discarded can help us sharpen our thinking, focus on neglected facts, and point us ultimately in the right direction. For this, they have earned our gratitude, if not necessarily our agreement.

The following survey divides these theories that link the scrolls and Christianity into two groups. The first group includes those hypotheses that see the pre-Christian Qumran sect as the true origin of characteristic Christian beliefs. The second group sees the Qumran sect as identical with the early church.

Christianity and the Essenes

People have been reading Josephus's and Philo's descriptions of the Essenes for almost two thousand years with intense interest. Some have felt that these pious, white-robed, celibate, pacifist, egalitarian monks were simply too good to be true. Others have felt that they were simply too good not to be Christians. The early church historian Eusebius, writing in the fourth century A.D., believed that Philo's Therapeutae, an Essene-like group, were actually early Christian monks. During the Reformation, Roman Catholics also argued that the Essenes were early Christian monks, hoping to prove the antiquity of the monastic orders that were under attack from the Protestants as a late innovation. However, it is clear that the Essenes existed before Christianity and therefore could not have been a Catholic monastic order.

The nineteenth-century English essayist Thomas de Quincey praised the Essenes as "a secondary Christianity not less spiritual, not less heavenly, not less divine than the primary."[3] Other writers of the eighteenth and nineteenth centuries who had been heavily influenced by the skepticism and rationalism of Deism claimed that Essenism was the true source of Christianity. They maintained variously that John the Baptist and Jesus were Essenes, and that all of their teaching reflected Essene doctrine. Since the New Testament contains no reference to the Essenes, they considered it a falsification of "what really happened."

This tendency reached its high (or low) point in the works of the nineteenth-century French scholar Ernest Renan. Renan completely disbelieved in miracles and the supernatural and attempted to explain Jesus and the rise of Christianity in purely human terms. The Essene communities were a "first rough sketch" of Christianity. He saw Jesus as a deluded Galilean peasant, while the Christianity of his followers was "an Essenism which has largely succeeded."

The Essene theory of Christian origins was so flawed that scholars had no difficulty in refuting it. By the turn of the nineteenth century, few serious scholars supported it.[4] But the discovery of the Dead Sea Scrolls revived it.

André Dupont-Sommer

The main mover in this revival was the French scholar André Dupont-Sommer (1900–1983). Dupont-Sommer was one of the first and loudest voices raised in support of the identification of the Qumran sect with the Essenes, and in fact, his arguments convinced most of those who studied the texts.

But Dupont-Sommer was also a devoted admirer of Ernest Renan. Like Renan, he had been a Catholic who had left the faith. Like Renan, he became an expert in ancient Hebrew and Aramaic. He eventually was appointed to the professorial chair at the Collège de France once held by Renan. Edmund Wilson even said that Dupont-Sommer "astonishingly resembles Renan. He is round-faced, short and rotund, bland and urbane and smiling."[5]

Dupont-Sommer, as a follower of Renan, believed he could put the explanation of Christianity as a "successful Essenism" back on its feet by his interpretations of the Dead Sea Scrolls. He accordingly read into them some similarities to Christianity that others have simply not been able to find. His most notable attempt was to interpret the enigmatic hints of the *Habbakuk Pesher* as pointing to an Essene belief in a Messiah who was persecuted, put to death, appeared in glory, and was to come again at the end of time. If this interpretation succeeded, then the Gospel stories could be seen as indebted to their Essene predecessors. It will be recalled that, in a mysterious passage, the "Wicked Priest" pursued the "Teacher of Righteousness":

> The Wicked Priest pursued the Teacher of Righteousness to destroy him in his hot anger in the place of his exile. And in the time appointed for the repose of the Day of Atonement, he appeared to

> them to destroy them and to overthrow them on the fast day of their Sabbath rest (XI, 4–8).

Most who read this passage see only one episode; but Dupont-Sommer sees two. The Wicked Priest, he says, pursued the Teacher to destroy him, and succeeded. The second sentence refers to a later event, wherein the glorified Teacher was believed to have revealed himself to his enemies after his death and destroyed them on the Day of Atonement. This second episode, says Dupont-Sommer, occurred during the capture of Jerusalem by the Roman Pompey on the Day of Atonement in 63 B.C.

Dupont-Sommer also sees the death of the Teacher in another place in the *Habakkuk Pesher*. The commentary deals with Habakkuk 2:7, "Will not your debtors suddenly arise? Will they not wake up and make you tremble? Then you will become their victim." The exposition begins at the bottom of what is left of Column VIII:

> The interpretation of the word concerns the priest who rebelled [*gap in scroll*] Laws of [God]. . .

Here the column breaks off. At the head of Column IX, the *pesher* continues:

> . . . to wound him with judgments of wickedness, and horrors of evil diseases they have executed on him and acts of revenge in the body of his flesh (IX, 1–2).

Dupont-Sommer argued that the latter passage refers to the tortures inflicted on the Teacher by the Wicked Priest. It is the "Passion" of the Teacher: "he suffered in 'his body of flesh': without doubt he was a divine being who 'became flesh' to live and die as a man."[6] Dupont-Sommer achieves this result by restoring some of the missing lines from the broken bottom of Column VIII: "the priest who rebelled [and violated] the Laws [of God and persecuted the Teacher of Righteousness]."

Most specialists disagreed with Dupont-Sommer's reading. In the first passage, there is no indication that the Teacher was killed, and it is most natural to take the phrase "he appeared to them to destroy them" as referring to the Wicked Priest, not the Teacher of Righteousness. And it is not clear at all how the "glorious reappearance" of the tortured Teacher is connected with the Pompey's arrival in Jerusalem. How can such a supernatural exploit be dovetailed with the approach of the hated Roman? Dupont-Sommer's understanding of this passage has little to recommend it.

The same is true of the passage that is supposed to narrate the "Passion of the Teacher." According to the "ground rules" of the commentary, the good figures of the prophecy are interpreted to be the Teacher and his followers, and the bad ones are the Teacher's enemies. Since Habakkuk 2:7 denounces the wicked, it is most natural to take the verse and its interpretation wholly as a reference to the fate of the Wicked Priest, not the Teacher. There is no reason to restore the missing lines as Dupont-Sommer did. It is the Priest, not the Teacher, who suffers the horrible diseases and the acts of vengeance in the "body of his flesh." (The latter phrase is an ordinary Hebrew expression referring to the human body. It has nothing to do with any "Incarnation.")

Although most of his peers in scholarship treated Dupont-Sommer with respect, giving his theories a fair hearing in many cases, his Renanesque explanation of the *Habakkuk Pesher* failed to gain many adherents. The same is true of a summary statement of his ideas about the Teacher and Jesus:

> The Galilean Master, as He is presented to us in the writings of the New Testament, appears in many respects as an astonishing reincarnation of the [Teacher]. Like the latter He preached penitence, poverty, humility, love of one's neighbour, chastity. Like him, He prescribed the observance of the Law of Moses, the whole Law, but the Law finished and perfected, thanks to His own revelations. *Like him He was the Elect and the Messiah of God, the Messiah redeemer of the world.* Like him He was the object of the hostility of the priests. . . . *Like him He was condemned and put to death.* Like him He pronounced judgement on Jerusalem. . . . *Like him, at the end of time, He will be the supreme judge. Like him He founded a Church whose adherents fervently awaited His glorious return.*[7]

The sentences emphasized are the ones I consider highly questionable. It is very unlikely that the sect considered the Teacher as the Messiah. Other texts from the scrolls plainly teach that the group still expected a Messiah who would save Israel (some passages even suggest that they expected two messiahs, a priestly Messiah and a royal Messiah). It is unlikely that the Teacher was executed, although he certainly was persecuted. There is no suggestion anywhere in the Dead Sea Scrolls that the Teacher, or any other human being, would be the supreme judge at the end of time. That role was assigned to God. Although the Teacher founded a group based on his teachings, there is no indication that his followers expected "his glorious return." Indeed, the comparison with Jesus Christ can only succeed if the Teacher formed the center of the sect's worship and devotions. He did not. Some of the scrolls, like the *War Scroll,* the *Manual of Discipline,* the *Temple Scroll,* and 4QMMT do not even mention the Teacher. He is not mentioned in any of the new Cave 4 material (with one possible exception).

In short, only the most general and vague likenesses can be discerned between the Teacher and Jesus of Nazareth. Most scholars were content to follow Dupont-Sommer's more justifiable suggestions about the Essene origin of the Dead Sea Scrolls and to leave his Christological speculations to one side.

The same cannot be said of some journalists and clergy who found Dupont-Sommer's "revelations" stimulating and sensational. The most prominent of these was the American Edmund Wilson.

Wilson (1895–1972) was a prominent leftist literary critic. Like Dupont-Sommer, he was an admirer of Renan and included a chapter on him in his enthusiastic account of the rise of communism, *To the Finland Station* (1937). Despite his agnosticism, Wilson had an interest in the Bible and in modern Israel, so when the Dead Sea Scrolls were discovered, he acquainted himself with their story and the men who were doing research on them. He conducted personal interviews with Dupont-Sommer, de Vaux, Yadin, the Archbishop Samuel, and other major figures. The result was a long piece in the May 1955 issue of the *New Yorker,* "A Reporter at Large: The Scrolls from the Dead Sea."

The article aroused considerable public interest in the scrolls, and when Wilson published a short book based on the article, *The Scrolls from the Dead Sea,* it was a best-seller for months. As Millar Burrows wryly remarked, "The Dead Sea Scrolls were discovered in America in the spring of 1955."[8]

Wilson tells a lively story, and his book is still well worth reading today for its picture of the early days of Qumran research.[9] But the most arresting parts of *The Scrolls from the Dead Sea* were the passages where Wilson enthusiastically champions Dupont-Sommer's Renanesque ideas about the Teacher of Righteousness. Wilson saw that an acceptance of Dupont-Sommer's interpretation would weaken Christianity's claims to be based on divine revelation. He welcomed this, and wondered whether Christian scholars

> may not have been somewhat inhibited in dealing with such questions as these by their various religious commitments. . . . [Christianity] may perfectly well be explained as the creation of several generations of Jews working by and for themselves. . . . One need not assume the miracle of a special magnanimous act of God to allow the salvation of the human race.[10]

Although scholars and specialists were at this time giving Dupont-Sommer's views the dispassionate examination they required—and coming to different conclusions—the public at large became either excited or dismayed. Scholars and nonspecialists began to write other books dealing with the controversy.

But other, less sensational books were published, including works by Cross, Burrows, and Milik. Their approach reflected more precisely the way scholars understood the scrolls. Eventually their ideas supplanted the more theatrical Wilsonian ones.

Dupont-Sommer never changed his basic notions. Despite the abiding value of many of his works, his attempt to link Essenism and Christianity remains an object lesson in how a particular private agenda can dictate a scholar's conclusions.

John Allegro

Chapter 2 discusses the role John Allegro played in reinforcing the idea that Christians were somehow suppressing the release of the Cave 4 texts. It was noted that Allegro himself could not be considered completely objective, both because of his own zealously antireligious perspective and his ambitions to take over the management of the scrolls.

Here I only want to discuss Allegro's interpretation of certain scrolls and his attempt to relate them to Christian beliefs. Like Dupont-Sommer, Allegro held to a pre-Christian dating of the scrolls and believed that the Qumran sectarians were the Essenes.

For Allegro, then, as for Dupont-Sommer, Essenism had to be a kind of "Christianity before Christ." Instead of using the *Habakkuk Pesher,* however, his main text was a text from his own lot, the fragmentary *Nahum Pesher*. The vital portion of that text reads as follows:

> "The lion killed enough for his cubs, and strangled the prey for his mate" (Nahum 2:12a) . . . the Angry Lion who smites by his great ones and the men of his party. . . . ["Filling with the kill] his lairs and his dens with the prey" (Nahum 2:12b) . . . acts of revenge against the "seekers of smoothness," who hangs up men alive . . . in Israel before, for concerning one hanged alive on a tree, it says, "Behold I am against you" (Nahum 2:13) (I, 4–9).

It is not at all clear who the Angry Lion and the "seekers of smoothness" are. Once again we are in the realm of the typically cryptic Qumranian interpretations.

Allegro deserves credit for figuring out exactly what is going on here. Based on some hints earlier in the text, he plausibly identified the "Angry Lion" with the Jewish king and high-priest Alexander Jannaeus, who reigned over Israel from 103 to 76 B.C. This Jannaeus was much hated by his subjects for his cruelty; some of them even went so far as to invite a foreign king Demetrius into the country to help them overthrow him. But after defeating Demetrius, Jannaeus took revenge on the Jewish rebels and crucified eight hundred of them—an event that Josephus records with horror (*The Jewish War* I.iv.6).

This event is probably cryptically referred to in the *Nahum Pesher*. The Jewish rebels are the "seekers of smoothness" that Jannaeus, the Angry Lion, "hangs up alive," crucifies them. This much makes sense, but Allegro goes a step further. The Angry Lion, he asserts, is also the Wicked Priest; and among those crucified by the Lion was the Teacher of Righteousness.

> [Jannaeus] descended on Qumran and arrested its leader, the mysterious "Teacher of Righteousness," whom he turned over to his mercenaries to be crucified. . . . When the Jewish king had left, [the sectarians] took down the broken body of their Master to stand guard over it until Judgment Day. For they believed that the terrible events of their time were surely heralding the visitation of God Himself. . . . They believed their Master would rise again and lead his faithful flock (the people of the new testament, as they called themselves) to a new and purified Jerusalem. . . . What is clear is that there was a well-defined Essenic pattern into which Jesus of Nazareth fits. What theologians make of that is really outside my province. I just give my findings.[11]

Anyone who compares the excerpt from the *Nahum Pesher* with the quote just given can see that Allegro's theory is very speculative. Not only this, but Allegro's reading of the excerpt demands that Jannaeus's enemies be the "seekers of smoothness," which were also the enemies of the sect, as the other scrolls make clear. Why would Jannaeus, who Allegro thinks is the persecutor of the sect, crucify the *enemies* of his own opponents? Why would the Teacher be crucified with the hated "seekers of smoothness"? Actually, the Teacher is never mentioned, nor is the Wicked Priest.

Allegro's statement led his colleagues to write a letter denouncing him (see p. 47). Allegro backed off, saying he had been misquoted. His own popular book on the scrolls soft-pedals his interpretation, saying that one should "avoid too dogmatic assertions about the life of the Teacher or the manner of his death."[12]

Still, Allegro never ceased to believe in his interpretation and continued to elaborate it in one of his last books, *The Dead Sea Scrolls and the Christian Myth* (1979). There he repeats his reading of the *Nahum Pesher* and adds to it the theory that the Essene sectarians encoded their secret doctrine (consisting of instructions for engaging in fertility rites) in a series of fictional narratives that later became known as the Gospels. The story of "Jesus" (a person who never existed) was derived from the life of the Qumran Teacher. Greeks uninitiated into Essene lore took the symbolic narratives for literal truth, and Christianity was born.

Allegro also published a final "bootleg" text of a small fragment, 4Q341, which he interpreted as an Essene medical text written in a kind of code. He regarded the text as directly confirming his theories. However, Israeli scholar Joseph Naveh pointed out that 4Q341 is actually a scribal writing exercise, in which a scribe practiced his letters by writing some letters of the alphabet, proper names from the Bible and elsewhere, and random collections of letters.[13] Only Allegro's imagination could find a text in that fragment.

John Allegro started out as a promising scholar. He made genuine contributions, in the beginning, to the understanding of the Dead Sea Scrolls. But his antireligious obsessions introduced confusion into the discussion and in the end clouded his own judgment. His accusations of prejudice and fear more accurately described his own mindset rather than those of his opponents; but he succeeded in arousing lasting suspicions of religious bias that, ultimately, only drew attention away from the real issues. That, regrettably, is his most enduring legacy.[14]

Christianity at Qumran

Dupont-Sommer and Allegro both accepted the consensus that the Dead Sea sectarians were Essenes, that the Dead Sea Scrolls were not themselves Christian writings, and that the scrolls could be dated archaeologically and paleographically to pre-Christian times. The writers discussed next challenge the consensus. They believe that the Dead Sea Scrolls were, in some sense, Christian writings or directly connected to Christian origins; they must therefore also challenge the pre-Christian dating of the majority of the scrolls.

Robert Eisenman and "Jamesian Christianity"

It is not insignificant that John Allegro is one of the few Qumran scholars that Robert Eisenman respects. He cherishes his own status as a maverick "opposition scholar" in the mold of Allegro. Eisenman played an important, if not decisive, role in the "rediscovery" of the scrolls and continues to issue publications in support of his own theory of the history of Qumran.

Eisenman's approach is indebted at many points to previous scroll scholars. He has recycled many of G. R. Driver's arguments against the archaeological and paleographical evidence for the dating of the scrolls. He connects the Qumran literature with the Zealot movement, *à la* Roth and Driver. He also wishes to see the Qumranians as "breakaway" Sadducees, along the lines proposed previously. But he connects these movements with the early Jewish-Christians in a way that is reminiscent of another early theorist, J. L. Teicher of Cambridge, who proposed that the Dead Sea Scrolls were written by the early Christian sect of Ebionites.[15] Finally, the connection of the Zealot movement with Christianity has long been bruited about, particularly in the sixties, when some proposed a "revolutionary Jesus."

But despite the derivative nature of much of his work, Eisenman produced, in the end, an original thesis: that James the Just, the brother of Jesus, is the Teacher of Righteousness, while the

Teacher's opponents, the Man of the Lie and the Wicked Priest are, respectively, the apostle Paul and the high priest Ananus, who presided over the execution of James in A.D. 62.[16]

Eisenman's view, developed over several books,[17] may be summarized as follows. When the Maccabean period ended in 63 B.C. with the supremacy of the Romans and the installation of Herod the Great as a puppet-ruler for Rome (37 B.C.), Israel's religious groups divided into two broad categories. One group was willing to collaborate with the Romans, Herod, and Herod's descendants. The other group opposed any kind of accommodation to Gentiles, fostering an ideal of perfect righteousness and purity that entailed hatred of all foreigners. They looked for a warlike Messiah who would eventually lead them in an eschatological showdown against the Gentiles and their Jewish collaborators. Eisenman believes the first group to have been the Sadducees and Pharisees, the second group the "breakaway" group of Sadducees, who were also the Essenes, who were also the Zealots.

The early Christian movement, according to Eisenman, belonged to the second group. John the Baptist began a general Messianic agitation after the death of Herod. Jesus of Nazareth in his own way contributed to this agitation and was eventually executed as a Zealot. Eventually James, Jesus' brother, took over leadership of the Zealot/Zadokite/Essene movement, expelling the accommodationist Paul from the group for propagating dangerous nonsense centering around Jesus. In an abortive attempt to take over the temple and celebrate rituals as "opposition" high priest, James was killed by the pro-Roman, high-priestly groups.

Eisenman believes there is evidence of this scenario in the Dead Sea Scrolls, the literature of this Zealot/Zadokite/Messianic movement. The scrolls are clearly the product of an "opposition" group. The sectarians opposed the current leaders of the nation; they looked for a Messiah who would lead them in battle; they maintained strict rules about purity; they opposed collaboration with Gentiles.

Eisenman's most controversial idea is his identification of James the Just as the Teacher and Paul with the Man of the Lie. Since the Teacher was a priest, called "righteous," and put to death by the high priest in Jerusalem, Eisenman argues that this points to James, who was also a priest, called "righteous," and put to death by a high priest in Jerusalem. Paul must be the Man of the Lie, since in his epistles he strenuously objects to being called a "liar" (e.g., 2 Cor. 11:31). Since the Man of the Lie is said in the *Habakkuk Pesher* to have rejected the laws of God and to have founded a "city in bloodshed," this also points to Paul, who founded an alternate movement ("a city") based on the blood of Christ and on faith "apart from the law." Eisenman says Paul was excommunicated by the Qumran Zealots/Zadokites for his heretical teachings.

Eisenman's theory can be challenged on many fronts. His selective use of sources is open to question, as well as his dating of the New Testament to the second century A.D. I will concentrate here on his interpretation of the scrolls themselves. Since he considers them as "eyewitness accounts" of the events with which they deal, his understanding of them is crucial to his case.

Eisenman believes that the *Habakkuk Pesher* refers to the martyrdom of James the Just in A.D. 62. According to Josephus, a man named Ananus became high priest while Judea was temporarily without a Roman governor; and Ananus, taking this opportunity to use his authority,

> assembled the sanhedrin of judges, and brought before them the brother of Jesus, who was called Christ, whose name was James, and some others; and when he had formed an accusation against them as breakers of the law, he delivered them to be stoned (*Antiquities* XX.ix.2).

Eisenman claims that this incident is described in the key passage of the *Habakkuk Pesher:*

> The Wicked Priest pursued the Teacher of Righteousness to destroy him in his hot anger in the place of his exile. And in the time appointed for the repose of the Day of Atonement, he appeared to them to destroy them and to overthrow them on the fast day of their Sabbath rest (XI, 4–8).

The two passages seem very different. In Josephus you find a wicked priest killing a righteous man, but that is clearly not enough to identify the two incidents. Eisenman attempts to reconcile them by recalling that, according to an ancient legend, James was a priest.[18] It was in James's role as rebel High Priest, says Eisenman, that he went to the temple to perform the ritual of the Day of Atonement.

There the accommodationist Ananus had him and his followers arrested and killed.

There are a number of flaws in Eisenman's scenario. The crucial element is the information that James was a priest and had access to the Holy of Holies. If this is rejected as a pious fiction, as most scholars believe it is, then the theory fails. We can also note, as we did in discussing Dupont-Sommer's interpretation of the same passage, that there is nothing in the *Pesher* to confirm the impression that the Wicked Priest actually succeeded in killing the Teacher.

The *Pesher* also mentions that the Wicked Priest "was called by the name of truth at the beginning of his service, but when he had ruled in Israel his mind became arrogant and he betrayed the Commandments for wealth" (VIII, 8–13). Could these terms apply to Ananus? According to Josephus, Ananus was high priest for only three months, and his action against James took place at the beginning of that time period. The *Habakkuk Pesher* seems to presuppose a longer period than that.

Eisenman finally asserts, without evidence, that James was tried on blasphemy:

> For his part, Josephus testifies that James was tried before a Pharisaic/Sadducean Sanhedrin on a charge of blasphemy, i.e., pronouncing or causing others to pronounce the forbidden name of God [as the high priest did on Yom Kippur].[19]

There is nothing like this in Josephus's narrative.

In short, Eisenman has to misread the *Pesher,* Josephus, and early church tradition in order to produce a narrative not contained in any source. His attempt to find a connection between James the Just and the Dead Sea Scrolls should accordingly be rejected.

The same applies to Eisenman's identification of Paul with the Man of the Lie. Eisenman argues that since Paul often states that he is not lying (as in 2 Cor. 11:31), he must have been accused of lying. Therefore he is the "Man of the Lie" of the Dead Sea Scrolls. This approach assumes (1) that the Qumran sect was the only group in the first century A.D. that called its principal opponent a liar, and (2) that Paul was the only religious controversialist that defended himself against such charges. This is not very convincing, and neither are Eisenman's other attempts to link Paul to particular passages in the scrolls.

Eisenman recognizes that the generally accepted limits of Qumran chronology stand in the way of his theory. If the scrolls were written at Qumran, and if they were hidden when Qumran was destroyed in A.D. 68, that would not leave much time for the *Habakkuk Pesher* to be written. James was killed in A.D. 62. The *Pesher* could have been written between 62 and 68, but the ink would still have been wet when it was placed in the cave.

Eisenman therefore places much weight on the arguments extending the time when the documents could have been written. G. R. Driver tried most of these out in the fifties and sixties (see pp. 110–11). These arguments have some merit, as already noted. If any part of Eisenman's theory survives scrutiny, it will most likely be this part. It is true that the paleographical evidence needs comprehensive rethinking. It is also true, as he argues, that there is no necessary reason to link the end of the Qumran settlement with the deposit of the scrolls. If the sectarians survived the end of their settlement—and why not?—that would give them more time to write texts like the *Habakkuk Pesher,* which, on Eisenman's theory, would likely date from some years after the end of the Jewish war.

However, poking holes in the prevailing view is not the same as setting up another theory. If the scroll sect actually lived at Qumran, as Eisenman believes, then where did they go? Eisenman suggests that they continued to live in caves, as they must have done before the destruction, since Khirbet Qumran is a community center with no living quarters. But if so, they must have done without the facilities provided by the buildings—the cisterns containing water for drinking and bathing, the pottery workshop, the smithy, the communal dining room, the scriptorium (if there was one), and so on. Would the sectarians have remained in the vicinity without these conveniences? Is it not more likely that, if they survived, they would relocate? And if they did move, why were most of the scrolls found in the vicinity of Khirbet Qumran? If they did put their scrolls in the caves after the war, why didn't they come back for them?

The most reasonable way to deal with all these questions is still to assume that the scrolls were deposited shortly before the Romans destroyed the installation at Qumran. The sect was broken by these events and their members scattered. We do not know for sure that this happened, but it makes sense, and it has not been disproved.

Eisenman also attempted to foil the "establishment" chronology by calling for new carbon-14 tests. Initial carbon-14 tests on the linen wrapping of the Cave 1 scrolls yielded a date of A.D. 33, plus or minus two hundred years. That result is too vague to be satisfying, since it only rules out extremist claims for the lateness of the scrolls.

But new methods have been developed since those early days. Carbon-14 tests can now be performed using the technique of Accelerator Mass Spectrometry (AMS), a technique requiring only tiny bits of tested matter to be reduced to carbon. The development of this technique opened the way for carbon-14 tests to be performed on samples taken from the scrolls themselves.

In 1989, Eisenman wrote Gen. Drori demanding AMS carbon-14 testing for the scrolls. He clearly expected the results would confirm his own dating for the scrolls. When the tests were finally run, the results confirmed the "establishment's" paleographical dating of the scrolls. Scientists at the Institut für Mittelenergiephysick in Zurich, the same ones who had tested the celebrated Shroud of Turin, were given fourteen samples. Eight were from the Qumran literature (including the *Temple Scroll,* the *Genesis Apocryphon,* the *Thanksgiving Scroll,* and the Cave 1 complete Isaiah scroll), and the other six samples were from other discoveries in the Judean desert that both preceded and followed the period of the Qumran scrolls. Four of the latter scrolls were chosen because they were dated by the scribes themselves.

The four dated scrolls confirmed the accuracy of the experiment: The dates yielded by the test dovetailed with the dates written in the scrolls. Of the eight undated scrolls, six produced dates that confirmed the paleographical estimates. The radiocarbon dates of the two remaining scrolls varied from the paleographic dating by 100–150 years in one case, and around 200 years in the second. The technicians suspected contamination in the latter case, though they were unable to find it.[20]

No one claims that the AMS carbon-14 tests are infallible. They are generally believed to be more accurate with papyrus documents than with leather ones like the Dead Sea Scrolls.[21]

Nevertheless, they do support the consensus dating of the scrolls established by paleography, archaeology, and textual analyis.

Not surprisingly, Eisenman has changed his mind about the importance of AMS carbon-14 tests. The process "is still in its infancy, subject to multiple variables, and too uncertain" to be useful, and the tests of the Swiss lab "were neither extensive enough nor secure enough" to provide definite dates.[22]

Barbara Thiering

Almost everyone has had a dream that begins in the surroundings of the everyday world, but ends in a bizarre fantasy world. The writings of Barbara Thiering of the University of Sydney, Australia, remind one of such dreams. Her studies[23] begin in the ordinary world of biblical scholarship but wind up in an eccentric universe of her own imagining. It is difficult to do more than give a brief summary of Thiering's approach and quite impossible to fit her into any of the prevailing pigeonholes for Qumran studies. Her theory is unique.

Thiering believes that the Qumran sect, whom she takes to be the Essenes, is the matrix from which the early church emerged. She identifies the Teacher of Righteousness with John the Baptist and his opponent, the Wicked Priest/Man of the Lie (for her they are the same) with Jesus of Nazareth. As remarkable as these identifications are, they are the least startling of all her conclusions.

According to Thiering's reconstruction, the Essene group split into two factions, one led by John, the other by Jesus. The Gospels and Acts come from the latter group. Since the Essenes interpreted the Old Testament prophets as secretly foretelling their own history in the *Pesher* commentaries, the Gospels must also be interpreted as coded Essene documents. They cannot be understood unless you know their secret language.

For instance, by reading the Gospels as a text concealing esoteric symbolism, Thiering claims that even the most innocuous words in the Gospels are laden with meaning. The word *all,* for instance, refers to the king Herod Agrippa I; *apostles* refers to John Mark; *crowds* also refers to Agrippa I, as does the expression *disciples of John; earthquake* refers to the head of the Egyptian branch of Essenes; *elders* means James the Just, as does *Joseph of Arimathea;*

Jews means the head of the circumcised Gentiles; *leper* and *lightning* refer to the heretic Simon Magus; *the Pharisees* equals the high priest Caiaphas; *Zacchaeus* is the high priest Ananus; and so on.[24]

Furthermore, all place names in the Gospels are taken to refer to geographical features of the Qumran area. Khirbet Qumran is *Jerusalem,* while *Jericho, Egypt, Red Sea, Capernaum,* and *Jordan* all refer to caves or ruins in the Qumran area. Terms like *Mount of Olives, Siloam, garden* and *Golgotha* all correspond to rooms or other features of Khirbet Qumran.[25]

With these assumptions, Thiering reconstructs the "true" Gospel events. Her method can be illustrated by her interpretation of the raising of Lazarus from the dead (John 11). In her eyes, the story is not about a man named Lazarus who died, was buried, and was raised to life by Jesus. It is about Simon Magus, the "pope" of the Zealots ("Lazarus") who was excommunicated by the Essenes ("he died") and symbolically interred in a cave near Qumran—Cave 4, to be exact. Jesus, who was a friend of Simon Magus, chose to release Simon from his confinement and went to Qumran. Simon's wife, Helena ("Martha"), met him and told him that "Lazarus," being dead, would "stink," that is, be ritually unclean. But Jesus went ahead anyway and released Simon, who emerged from Cave 4 still wearing his high priestly garb ("graveclothes").

This method sometimes leads Thiering to suppress facts. For instance, she states that scholars found "copies of some of the gospels" at Khirbet Mird, about five miles inland from Khirbet Qumran. Therefore, she claims that Mird and Qumran were part of the same Christian organization. "The party that met at Mird was westernized, and became Christian, while the men who met at Qumran were those who remained Jewish."[26] But presumably Thiering knows perfectly well that Khirbet Mird is the site of a Christian monastery that was established in A.D. 492, more than five hundred years after the Dead Sea Scrolls were written. Its gospels date from the fifth to the eighth centuries A.D.

Other elementary questions keep occurring to the reader. If they had such a passion for secrecy, why did they sometimes use real names and other times code names? And why did the Gospel writers use such bizarre Greek? For instance, every beginning seminarian knows about the emphatic negative *ou mé,* "by no means." But Thiering, contrary to two thousand years of the study of Greek, takes it to be a double negative, therefore an emphatic positive, since "all words must be accounted for."[27] (This would mean, by the way, that John the Baptist would "most emphatically [*ou mé*] drink wine and other fermented drink" [Luke 1:15], a fact that contradicts the rest of Thiering's theory about him.)

There is, of course, no evidence that the New Testament was written as a code for the Essenes. The only evidence Thiering offers is the probability of her reconstructions. Most scholars, liberal and conservative, have not been impressed. Even secularists will find it hard to believe that the Gospels were simply a "front" for Essene internal history.

Theiring's motive seems to be to provide a method to bolster her rationalistic reconstructions of the Gospel miracles. She cannot believe in the literal truth of the resurrection and other miracles. She has this in common with other skeptics. But, unlike them, she cannot believe that they were intended to be taken seriously. They must have a hidden meaning. Even her fellow rationalists, however, may find the miracles easier to believe than her Byzantine reinterpretations of them, especially when she weirdly accepts the inerrancy of Scripture as "a useful working hypothesis"![28]

Jose O'Callaghan

More ink has been spilled discussing the ideas of Father Jose O'Callaghan than the previous four authors put together. His theories are fundamentally different from the others we have looked at in that they are not directed, implicitly or explicitly, against Christian beliefs. But O'Callaghan belongs here because his proposals, if true, support a connection between the Dead Sea Scrolls and the early church. Indeed, they can (and have) been used to support certain traditionally conservative positions on an early dating of the Gospel of Mark and other New Testament documents. It is therefore unfortunate, from one point of view, that O'Callaghan's proposals are so unlikely to be true.

O'Callaghan, a Spanish Jesuit and expert in the study of ancient papyrus documents, published a paper in 1972 proposing to identify a scrap of papyrus found in Cave 7 (7Q5) as a fragment of the Gospel of Mark.[29] Although O'Callaghan's suggestion—and his further claims to having identified bits of Acts, Romans, 1 Timothy, James, and 2 Peter—was advanced modestly enough, scholars received it for what it was, a bombshell that threatened to explode any number of long-held theories about when the New Testament was written, where, and by whom.

How could "one small fragment shake the world"?[30] All of the New Testament texts were written between about A.D. 50 and 100. Many scholars today tend to date the majority of New Testament texts closer to the end of that period and attribute their composition, by and large, to gentile Christians outside Palestine, not Jewish Christians in Palestine. If O'Callaghan is right, then the composition of Mark's Gospel—usually dated around A.D. 65 in Rome—would have to be moved back to an earlier time (A.D. 50) and a different place (Palestine). The other New Testament books would have to undergo similar reevaluations. Many scholars do not consider 2 Peter, for instance, to have come from the hand of Peter, but from an anonymous disciple perhaps as late as the early second century A.D. O'Callaghan's thesis would consign that theory to the dustbin of history.

The popular evangelical and Catholic press happily used O'Callaghan's theories to lambast liberal scholarship. *Eternity* magazine predicted that "all contemporary Barthian and Bultmannian views of the New Testament's formation will come crashing down in one inglorious heap." The *National Catholic Reporter,* in a similar vein, said that now "they can make a bonfire of 70 tons of indigestible German scholarship," while *Christianity Today* hailed the find as a "biblical breakthrough." Some specialists were impressed as well; Prof. Bruce Metzger of Princeton, an expert on the New Testament text, admitted that 7Q5 indeed "appears to be from a very ancient copy of Mark."[31]

Nevertheless, most scholars, liberal and conservative, had and continue to have grave reservations about O'Callaghan's methods and conclusions. For one thing, 7Q5 is a tiny fragment preserving traces of about twenty Greek letters, only about ten of them clearly. O'Callaghan claimed to read part of Mark 6:52–53 in this postage-stamp-sized scrap. The words preserved on the fragment are capitalized in the following English translation; the line breaks follow O'Callaghan's proposals:

> [had not understood] A[bout the loaves;]
> [but t]HEIR H[earts were harden-]

[e]D. AND W[hen they had crossed over,]
[they landed at Ge]NNES[aret and]
[ancho]RED [there. As soon as]

Only one entire word is legible, the word ***and*** (Greek: ***kai***). Furthermore, many specialists felt that O'Callaghan had misread several of the letters on the fragment, especially in the second, third, and fifth lines, reducing the legible parts of the fragment to something like this:

[. . . . .]
[. . . . .]HE[. . . . .]
[. . . . . . .] AND W[. . . . .]
[. . . . .]NNE[. . . . .]
[. . . . .]ED[. . . . .]

Now obviously it would not be too difficult to come up with different sentences that would fit these traces, and O'Callaghan's critics did so, finding a number of verses in the Septuagint that fit the remaining letters and those of the other fragments. They established that O'Callaghan's reconstructions were not the only ones possible.

Not only that, but O'Callaghan had to depart from the Greek text of Mark in order to find it in 7Q5. To come up with "and when they crossed over" in Greek, he had to omit three words in the original text. Literally translated, the Greek text as we have it says "to the land they came, to Gennesaret." O'Callaghan's reconstructed text does not have the words "to the land." Every biblical manuscript, like all ancient texts, differs from the next in minor ways, so it is possible that one text might have omitted these words. But of all the hundreds of manuscripts of the Gospels, O'Callaghan's reconstruction is the only one lacking these words in Mark.

Another suspicious feature of O'Callaghan's reconstruction is that a word is spelled differently from the way it is in the standard text.[32] Again, this possibility cannot be ruled out. But scholars felt, and rightly, that if O'Callaghan was going to ask them to accept new and sensational claims about the date and location of New Testament texts, he ought not also to ask them to believe that it was a form of the text that no one had seen before.

Questions were also raised about the location of the find. Cave 7, like Cave 4, is quite close to Khirbet Qumran. Presumably it was one of the caves used by the sectarians. If they were not Christians, what were they doing with New Testament texts? One of O'Callaghan's defenders proposed that Cave 7, which contained only Greek texts, was actually used by Christians after the fall of Qumran. That is a possibility. But if true, it undercuts the significance of the identification, since Christians could have brought texts into the cave well after the end of the first century A.D. or the beginning of the second. That would indeed make them very early New Testament texts, but it would also allow most of the generally accepted datings of the Gospels and other texts to stand.

Most specialists, then, rapidly returned a verdict of "not proven" to O'Callaghan's identifications. If tons of German scholarship is to go up in smoke, it will not be O'Callaghan's match that starts the bonfire. Jerry Vardaman's summary from 1973 is worth repeating: "What we have thus far may be only *figments* of the imagination instead of *fragments* of the New Testament."[33]

O'Callaghan has never retracted his views, however, and one German scholar, C. P. Thiede, has recently come to his support.[34] But generally the ruling on O'Callaghan's proposals remains where it was twenty years ago. Further evidence would have to be brought forward to force any widespread reevaluation. So far there has been none.[35]

Conclusion

To devote a chapter to the ideas discussed here is to give them more attention than many specialists feel they deserve. I have done so because people are interested in these proposals, and they have attracted a lot of attention. Also, the authors mentioned (except for O'Callaghan) have in different ways accused the "establishment" of being biased against their views and of trying to "protect" the church from the truth. This accusation must be taken seriously. Evangelicals, whose perspective has often been disregarded in modern biblical scholarship, know that it is all too easy for a clique of scholars to impose a point of view on a field of study while neglecting worthy ideas from outside the approved circle.

In Qumran studies, however, the sound of grinding axes has usually come from the antireligious side. Accusing religious scholars of defensive reactions in the face of inconvenient facts is a popular rhetorical move nowadays; but as far as the Dead Sea Scrolls are concerned, the facts are mainly inconvenient for the other side.

Notes

1. Krister Stendahl, "The Scrolls and the New Testament: An Introduction and a Perspective," in *The Scrolls and the New Testament,* ed. K. Stendahl (1957; reprint, New York: Crossroad, 1992), 1.

2. Burrows, *More Light on the Dead Sea Scrolls,* 39.

3. Thomas de Quincey, "The Essenes," *Historical and Critical Essays* (Boston: N.p., 1853), 116.

4. Siegfried Wagner, *Die Essener in der Wissenschaftlichen Diskussion von Ausgang des 18. bis zum Beginn des. 20. Jahrhunderts* (The Essenes in Scientific Discussion from the End of the 18th to the Beginning of the 20th Century) (Berlin: Alfred Töpelmann, 1960), 228–31. Bishop J. B. Lightfoot's comment is typical: "Thus at whatever point we test the teaching and practice of our Lord by the characteristic tenets of Essenism, the theory of affinity fails" (*Saint Paul's Epistles to the Colossians and to Philemon* [London: N.p., 1890], 413).

5. Wilson, *The Scrolls from the Dead Sea,* 100.

6. André Dupont-Sommer, *The Dead Sea Scrolls: A Preliminary Survey* (Oxford: Blackwell, 1952), 34. This book is an English translation of *Aperçus préliminaires sur les manuscrits de la Mer Morte* (Paris, 1950).

7. Dupont-Sommer, *Dead Sea Scrolls,* 99.

8. Burrows, *More Light on the Dead Sea Scrolls,* 3.

9. Wilson continued to revise the book in later years. He added several chapters to bring readers up-to-date in *The Dead Sea Scrolls 1947–1969* (1970), and several more pieces about the Bible and Israel were added to make *Israel and the Dead Sea Scrolls* (New York: Farrar, Straus & Giroux, 1978).

10. Wilson, *Scrolls from the Dead Sea,* 98–99.

11. *Time* magazine, 6 February 1956: as quoted by J. Fitzmyer, *Responses to 101 Questions on the Dead Sea Scrolls* (New York: Paulist, 1992), 164.

12. John Allegro, *The Dead Sea Scrolls: A Reappraisal* (New York: Penguin, 1964), 109. This volume is a revised edition of Allegro's original book published in 1956. Edmund Wilson and Allegro, who might have been expected to find much in common, actually had little respect for each other. Wilson accused Allegro of misleading the public, making "fantastic" conjectures, and resorting to "extremely far-fetched" methods (*Israel and the Dead Sea Scrolls,* 273–76). Allegro in turn referred in letters to "this nonsense of Wilson" (*Dead Sea Scrolls Deception,* 49).

13. Joseph Naveh, "A Medical Document or a Writing Exercise? The So-called 4Q Therapeia," *Israel Exploration Journal* 36 (1986): 52–55. An

American scholar, James Charlesworth, who had endorsed Allegro's interpretation had the embarrassing obligation to retract his opinions after Naveh's article came out.

14. Allegro's activities after the completion of his work for the Cave 4 team are worth a brief note. His volume of *Discoveries in the Judean Desert* came out in 1968. In 1970, he published *The Sacred Mushroom and the Cross,* in which he argued that Christianity was in its origin a fertility cult that made use of hallucinogenic drugs compounded from certain species of mushrooms. The name "Jesus" in the Gospels was in fact a cipher for this mushroom.

Allegro's reputation never recovered from this book. Later in 1970, he published *The End of a Road,* in which he, believing he had dealt the church a mortal blow in the previous book, imagined a world without Christianity. His later works include *The Chosen People* (1972), in which he attempts to account for Judaism by the same "fertility-mushroom" cult previously described and in such terms that many reviewers deemed it anti-Semitic; *The Dead Sea Scrolls and the Christian Myth* (1979); and *All Manner of Men* (1982), in which Allegro surveys the biological differences among the human races and concludes that racial segregation is a desirable method of controlling racial conflict. (The last book is copyrighted 1982, but datable on internal grounds to the early seventies.)

15. Teicher, in a series of articles published in the early fifties, contended that the Teacher of Righteousness was Jesus and that the Wicked Priest was Paul. Although other scholars recognized some kind of link between the Ebionites and Qumran, no one accepted Teicher's theory as he expressed it. Teicher never argued at length for the Teacher's identification with Jesus; he just assumed it.

16. Even this theory was foreshadowed in A. Powell Davies, *Meaning of the Dead Sea Scrolls* (New York: New American Library, 1956), 114–15.

17. *Maccabees, Zadokites, Christians and Qumran* (Leiden: Brill, 1983); *James the Just in the Habakkuk Pesher* (Leiden: Brill, 1986); and *The Dead Sea Scrolls Uncovered,* with Michael Wise (New York: Element, 1992).

18. Hegesippus states that James "alone was permitted to enter the Holy Place. . . . He used to enter the Sanctuary alone, and was often found on his knees beseeching forgiveness for the people" (see Eusebius, *The History of the Church* II.xxiii.11, trans. G. A. Williamson [Penguin, 1965; rev. ed. 1989]: 59). Eisenman says in a number of places that "early Christian sources" unanimously attribute to James the Just a priestly role. In fact, the third-century Ebionite *Ascents of James* states that "James spoke against the Temple and the sacrifices and against the fire of the altar" (cf. *The Writings of Paul,* ed. Wayne Meeks [New York: Norton, 1972], 177).

Hegesippus, by the way, says that James's accusers and assassins were the "scribes and Pharisees," not the Sadducee high priest Ananus, who is not mentioned. Eisenman has to combine Josephus's story of the death of James (which mentions Ananus and says that James was arrested for violation of the Jewish law, but makes no mention of James as priest) with Hegesippus's (which mentions James's priestly role, states that he was killed for preaching Christ as Savior, and does not mention Ananus) to produce a story that appears nowhere in any source.

19. Eisenman, *James the Just,* 62.

20. .Bonani et al., "Radiocarbon Dating of the Dead Sea Scrolls," *Atiqot* 20 (1991): 27–32. The radiocarbon dates of the Isaiah scroll are 202–107 B.C.; of the *Temple Scroll,* 97–1 B.C.; of the *Genesis Apocryphon,* 73 B.C.–14 A.D.; of the *Thanksgiving Scroll,* 21–61 B.C.

21. Thomas C. Lynn, "Dating Papyrus Manuscripts by the AMS Carbon-14 Method," *Biblical Archaeologist* (September 1988): 141–42.

22. Eisenman and Wise, *The Dead Sea Scrolls Uncovered,* 13.

23. Thiering's books are *Redating the Teacher of Righteousness* (1979), *The Gospels and Qumran* (1981), *The Qumran Origins of the Christian Church* (1983), and *Jesus and the Riddle of the Dead Sea Scrolls* (New York: HarperCollins, 1992). The last book is a summary of her thought for the general public.

24. *Jesus and the Riddle of the Dead Sea Scrolls,* 384–98.

25. Ibid., 284–331.

26. Ibid., 39.

27. Ibid., 379.

28. Ibid., 179.

29. Jose O'Callaghan, "¿Papiros neotestamentarios en la cueva 7 de Qumran?" (New Testament Papyri in Cave 7 of Qumran?) *Biblica* 53 (1972): 91–100. Fragment 7Q5 was originally published by Maurice Baillet in *DJD* 3.

30. See the anonymous article "Could One Small Fragment Shake the World?" *Eternity* 23/6 (1972): 1–14.

31. The quotations all appear in J. A. Fitzmyer, "A Qumran Fragment of Mark?" *America* 126/25 (24 June 1972): 649–50.

32. The words translated as "when they had crossed over" are a single word in Greek, the plural aorist participle DIAPERASANTES. Where this word should occur in 7Q5, according to O'Callaghan, we have only the letter *T,* possibly followed by *I,* and then it breaks off: TI[. . . . .]. O'Callaghan presumed a scribal error and restored TIAPERASANTES.

33. Jerry Vardaman, "The Gospel of Mark and 'The Scrolls,'" *Christianity Today* 17/25 (1973): 1287.

34. Thiede's 1986 book in German has been translated into English as *The Earliest Gospel Manuscript? The Qumran Fragment 7Q5 and Its Significance for New Testament Studies* (Exeter, England: Paternoster, 1992). S. R. Pickering and R. R. E. Cook have responded to Thiede in *Has a Fragment of the Gospel of Mark Been Found at Qumran?* (Sydney: Ancient History Documentary Research Centre, Macquarie University, 1989).

35. One scholar has recently suggested that 7Q4, which O'Callaghan wanted to identify with 1 Timothy 3:16–4:3, is actually a fragment from a Greek translation of the *Book of Enoch;* see G.-W. Nebe, "7Q4—Möglichkeit und Grenze einer Identifikation" (7Q4—Possibility and Limits of an Identification), *Revue de Qumran* 13 (1988): 629–33. A bibliography relating to O'Callaghan's identifications can be found in Joseph Fitzmyer's *Dead Sea Scrolls: Major Publications and Tools for Study,* rev. ed. (Atlanta: Scholars Press, 1992), 168–72.

Chapter 8

The Scrolls and the Gospels

Numerous parallels between the Qumran texts and the New Testament have been proposed. Some stem from an ardent desire to make the new discoveries explain everything. This desire has aptly been called "pan-Qumranism." But the New Testament and the Qumran texts were written out of the same culture and in roughly the same era. It is natural that expressions, ideas, and vocabulary "in the air" at the time should be employed in both literatures. In some cases, the Qumran writings can provide a generously detailed textual background for the New Testament writings.

It would be impossible to survey here all of the proposed connections. Entire books have been written on the subject.[1] I can only summarize in the broadest possible way the parallels that many scholars consider convincing. In addition, I want to highlight two areas of particular interest, the languages of Jesus and the teaching of the scrolls about the Messiah.

A typical list of important New Testament topics that the scrolls have illumined would include these:

Eschatology. The Qumran sect, like John the Baptist, Jesus, and the early Christians, believed their age was a decisive one, foretold by the prophets; and that they had to prepare themselves for God's intervention on the side of the righteous.

Criticism of Riches. An important part of early Christian doctrine is also prominent in the Dead Sea Scrolls: "the love of money is a root of all kinds of evil" (1 Tim. 6:10). At Qumran this led to compulsory communal sharing of money and property; in the early church, voluntary sharing was common and encouraged (Acts 2:44–45). The Old Testament is the ultimate source of the conviction of the corrupting power of money.

Theological Terminology. The Dead Sea Scrolls' usage of such terms as "mystery," "flesh," "spirit," "power," "truth," "light and darkness," and so on, have shown to scholars new shades of meaning in the writings of Paul and John. They have also shown that the Pauline Epistles and the Gospel of John are best interpreted in light of their Jewish background, and not solely in terms of their connections to Greco-Roman culture.

The Necessity of Conversion. For mainstream Judaism, physical descent from the patriarchs was enough for membership in God's covenant community, and obedience to the Law was enough to win his favor. The Qumran sect and the early Christians both believed that repentance and a conscious choice of Light over Darkness, Truth over Falsehood, was necessary for salvation. For the Qumranians, Light and Truth were found in the Torah as interpreted by the Teacher; for the early church, they were found in Jesus Christ.

The kind of Judaism represented at Qumran therefore furnishes a meaningful part of the background of the New Testament. Other "Judaisms" also provide important parallels. Rabbinic Judaism and Christianity are like each other and unlike Qumran at a number of points. The emphasis on resurrection of the dead is one instance; the use of parables in teaching is another; the concern for common people still another. Jewish and non-Jewish writings from outside Palestine are also crucial for understanding the environment of the New Testament writers.[2] The New Testament can be more richly understood when all the background information, not just a part, is taken into account.

The Language(s) of Jesus

One of the most promising new angles on the New Testament that the scrolls offer is fresh insight into the languages of Palestine from 200 B.C.–A.D. 100.

Most of the scrolls are written in the classical biblical dialect of Hebrew, the principal language of the Old Testament. At least three of the scrolls are written in the more colloquial, postbiblical dialect called "Mishnaic Hebrew"[3]: the *Copper Scroll*, 4QMMT, and a still unpublished pseudepigraphic fragment (4Q229).

A large number of scrolls are written in Aramaic, a language distinct from but related to Hebrew. A few of these are in the Nabatean dialect, but most are in Palestinian Aramaic. Finally, there are a few scrolls containing parts of the Septuagint, the earliest Greek translation of the Old Testament.

The presence of these three languages among the scrolls is rich with implication for the study of the Bible and especially the New Testament.

Before the discovery of the Dead Sea Scrolls, virtually no writings in Hebrew or Aramaic from 200 B.C.–A.D. 100 had been found. Most of those that survived are translations into Greek or other non-Semitic languages. This "Semitic silence" was relieved only by brief inscriptions on ossuaries or tombstones. The first real break in the silence came with the manuscript discoveries from the Cairo Geniza in the 1890s, which gave back to the world a Hebrew version of the ancient apocryphal book of Ecclesiasticus, an Aramaic version of the pseudepigraphic *Testament of Levi*, and the Hebrew *Damascus Document*. But since these books appeared in medieval copies that had been contaminated with the grammar and vocabulary of later dialects, many scholars doubted that they were truly ancient.

The Qumran finds changed all that. The "Semitic silence" became a "Semitic cacophony" as the voices of ancient Palestine were heard again. Perhaps the most surprising fact, at least to gentile scholars, was the prevalence of Hebrew in the scrolls. Before Qumran, it was often taken for granted that Aramaic was by far the most common language among Jews and that knowledge of Hebrew was on the decline. Some Jewish scholars had argued that Hebrew was still alive in this period. They pointed to the clear signs that some of the intertestamental books (like 1 Maccabees) were originally written in Hebrew. They also maintained that Mishnaic Hebrew was a spoken language, not an artificial scholarly creation from a later period as some had claimed.

The Dead Sea Scrolls vindicated these scholars. In the wake of the Qumran discoveries, some researchers even concluded that Hebrew was the sole language of Jews in the first century A.D. making it the language spoken by Jesus and the disciples. There is a body of scholars in Jerusalem, the so-called Jerusalem School of Synoptic Research, that assumes that Jesus spoke only Hebrew and that the earliest form of the Gospels was in Hebrew. This research angle would not have been possible before 1947.

Nevertheless, the language diversity has raised more questions than it has answered. Since the Dead Sea Scrolls appear to be the library of a particular sect, it is possible that their use of Hebrew was a group quirk not shared by outsiders. Another assessment of the situation is that Hebrew was still used for literary composition, but not for ordinary everyday speech, since most of the scrolls are written in the classical, not the colloquial, dialect.

So although the scrolls have established that three languages were in use in first-century Palestine, they have not shown who used them, or when, or how, or in what proportions. Milik thought that the scrolls prove "beyond reasonable doubt" that Mishnaic Hebrew was the normal spoken language.[4] Joseph Fitzmyer, by contrast, argues that

> the most commonly used language of Palestine in the first century A.D. was Aramaic, but that many Palestinian Jews . . . used Greek, at least as a second language. . . . But pockets of Palestinian Jews also used Hebrew, even though its use was not widespread.[5]

Most specialists agree with Fitzmyer, but there is no consensus. The real question is: What difference does it make? For New Testament scholars who seek to reconstruct the original words of Jesus, it makes a tremendous difference. Much of modern New Testament research is based on the likelihood that the Jews were monolingual. If they were actually bilingual, or even trilingual (Hebrew, Aramaic, and Greek), then much of this work will have to be done over. For instance, some scholars assume that the hymn in Luke 1:46–55 was not composed by Mary, but written by the Gospel writer in Greek in imitation of the Septuagint. The style is like the Psalms, but "everyone knows" that Hebrew poetry was no longer composed in

Mary's time. Yet it can be shown that the style of the hymn is like that of the *Thanksgiving Scroll* and uses the same poetic devices,[6] and so could plausibly have been uttered by a first-century Palestinian Jew like Mary.

But perhaps the most important fact is not which language was dominant, but simply the fact that Palestinian Jews wrote books in their own language—a fact that has implications for New Testament scholars. Before Qumran, it was possible to utter opinions such as this one by Edgar Goodspeed:

> The Gospel is Christianity's contribution to literature. It is the most potent type of religious literature ever devised. To credit such a creation to the most barren age of a never very productive tongue like Aramaic would seem the height of improbability.
>
> For in the days of Jesus the Jews of Palestine were not engaged in writing books. It is not too much to say that a Jerusalem or Galilean Jew of the time of Christ would regard writing a book in his native tongue with positive horror. . . . Jerusalem had neither the will nor the skill to produce the Gospels. No one has ever succeeded in fitting them into its literature or its life.[7]

Goodspeed lived to see his confident statements spectacularly exploded. It is now apparent that Jerusalem surely had both the skill and the will to produce native literature; whether the Gospels were among them is debatable—and yet more probable than it seemed before.

Unfortunately, many New Testament scholars still seem to be living in Goodspeed's pre-Qumran world, where the knowledge of Hebrew and Aramaic is negligible, and only Greek writings are relevant. The fact of a lively native literary culture in the first century A.D. has not had the impact it ought to have had. It is now possible to imagine the Gospel traditions being put into writing much earlier than ever before thought likely. If this possibility were accepted, it would demolish more German (and American) scholarship than O'Callaghan's textual speculations. For that very reason, it is unlikely that it will make much headway.

The Messiah and the Dead Sea Scrolls

A feature of the Dead Sea Scrolls that continues to draw attention is their messianic doctrine, both because of its intrinsic interest for Christians and because of the hasty claims some scholars have made about new messianic texts.

The word *Messiah* is derived from the Hebrew verb meaning "to anoint." In the Old Testament, people were anointed with oil as an initiation rite into the office of prophet, priest, or king. A "messiah" (*mashiah*) is therefore any "anointed one" who has been thus initiated.

The word *messiah,* "anointed," is not always a technical term referring to the Messiah. The "anointed priest," for instance, figures in the sacrificial ritual in Leviticus (e.g., Lev. 4:3, 5, 16). Elisha was anointed to succeed Elijah (1 Kings 19:16; see also Ps. 105:15). Kings of Israel and other countries were anointed to the royal office: Saul (1 Sam. 24:6), David (1 Sam. 16:13), Hazael (1 Kings 19:15), Jehoahaz (2 Kings 23:30), and so on. Even a world leader like Cyrus king of Persia can be referred to as "God's anointed" (Isa. 45:1). There is a tendency to use the word chiefly of the king of Israel or Judah; the "Lord's anointed" is almost always the legitimate king (e.g., 1 Sam. 2:10; Ps. 2:2, 18:50, 20:6, 132:10), especially from David's line.

The last mentioned usage, the Davidic king, leads into the technical usage of *Messiah* that New Testament readers are already familiar with. The Old Testament prophets foresaw a golden age for Israel when her various trials, punishments, exiles, and tribulations were over. This time of redemption would begin with the restoration of the monarchy through a righteous king from the line of David, whose reign would be characterized by peace, prosperity, blessings of every kind, submission of the Gentiles, and a renewal of the people's close relationship to God. Isaiah speaks of the Prince of Peace (9:1–7), the Branch/Root of Jesse (11: 1–10), the Leader of the Peoples (55:3–5), while Micah speaks of the shepherd ruler from Bethlehem (5:1–5). Jeremiah foretells the Righteous Branch (23:5–6; 33:15), Ezekiel the Davidic prince (34:23–24; 37:24–28), Zechariah the king of Zion (9:9–10).

In the Old Testament the term "God's anointed" and the blessed reign of David's descendant come close but never quite meet. The Branch of David is not called the Messiah in the Old Testament.[8] The first sources to make the connection explicit come from the intertestamental literature. Most notable is a collection of poems called the *Psalms of Solomon,* written in Israel after the Roman takeover in 63 B.C.

> See, Lord, and raise up for them their king, the son of David, to rule over your servant Israel in the time known to you, O God. Undergird him with the strength to destroy the unrighteous rulers, to purge Jerusalem from gentiles. . . .
>
> There will be no unrighteousness among them in his days, for all shall be holy, and their king shall be the Lord Messiah.[9]

In this quotation, a nonbiblical development is apparent: that the Messiah would militarily "destroy the unrighteous rulers" and lead Israel to victory over its foes. Such a concept of the Messiah—a descendant of David who would defeat the unrighteous in war, purge the Holy Land of Gentiles, and bring in, with God's help, the "Kingdom of God," a new era of peace and blessing—was prominent in Judaism in the first few centuries B.C. and A.D. It is plain from the histories of Josephus that several revolutionary leaders during the Roman period claimed to be the Messiah or were thought by their followers to be the Messiah.[10] This concept could invite the most violent images, as seen in this extract from a targum, an Aramaic paraphrase of Scripture:

> How beautiful are the eyes of the King Messiah who is to arise from the House of Judah! He girds his loins and goes out to war against his enemies, and kills kings and rulers, reddening the mountains with the blood of their slain, whitening the hills with the fat of their warriors. His garments are stained with blood, like one who treads grapes.[11]

But other images were also available, more in keeping with the Old Testament emphasis on peace. Another targum on Genesis 49:11 reads, "Israel shall surround his [the Messiah's] city, they shall build his temple. The righteous shall be round about him, those who do the Torah shall study with him."[12] Here the Messiah is a kind of super-rabbi, promulgating the true Law.

The Dead Sea Scrolls contain both kinds of messianic conceptions. The text 4Q252, part of a commentary on Genesis, interprets Genesis 49:10 straightforwardly as referring to the "Messiah of Righteousness, the Branch of David, to him and his seed is given the covenant of kingship." The text 4Q174, known as the *Florilegium,* quotes God's promise to David that he would build

David a house, raise up his seed after him, and establish the throne of his kingdom, becoming a father to the king, who would be called God's son (2 Sam. 7:11–14).

> This is the Branch of David, who will appear with the Interpreter of the Law in Zion in the latter days, as it is written: "I will restore David's fallen tent" (Amos 9:11). "David's fallen tent" is he who will arise to deliver Israel (4Q174 I, 11–13).

The Branch of David also appears in the *Isaiah Pesher*. The text quotes Isaiah 11:1–4, which speaks of the reign of the "shoot of Jesse"—which, as noted above, is a basic messianic text—and comments on it as follows:

> The interpretation of the text concerns the Branch of David, who will arise in the latter days [. . .] his enemies; God will support him [. . .] in the Torah . . . he shall rule over all the Gentiles . . . his sword shall judge the peoples (Fragment 8–10, 17–20).

Then the text quotes the verse from Isaiah 11:3: "He will not judge by what he sees with his eyes, or decide by what he hears with his ears." The scroll is fragmentary, but it interprets this verse to mean that the Messiah will be advised by priests: "As they instruct him, thus shall he rule; and at their word [. . .] With him one of the renowned priests shall go out."

The Prince of the Congregation

The Branch of David is one of the sect's most common names for the Davidic Messiah. Unlike the rabbinic texts quoted above, the sectarians did not like to call the Messiah a king, but they did refer to him sometimes as the Prince of the Congregation. The Hebrew word translated "prince" (or "ruler") is *nasi* and was used by the prophet Ezekiel in his messianic prophecies (34:23–34; 37:24–28).

The Prince of the Congregation appears in the *Damascus Document,* in the interpretation on Numbers 24:17: "A star will come out of Jacob; a scepter will rise out of Israel."

> The "star" is the Interpreter of the Law. . . . The "scepter" is the Prince of the whole Congregation. When he appears "he will smash all the sons of Sheth" (VII, 18–21) (Num. 24:17).

The title "Prince of the Congregation" is used when the scrolls want to emphasize the Messiah's warrior status, as in the *War Scroll,* the *Isaiah Pesher,* and most notably in the "Blessing for the Prince of the Congregation," found in the *Rule of Blessings:*

> A blessing for the Prince of the Congregation. . . . By the breath of your lips may you slay the wicked. . . . May God make your horns of iron and your hooves of bronze; may you gore like a bull and trample the Gentiles like mud in the streets (V, 24–27).

The most controversial text mentioning the Prince of the Congregation is the recently published 4Q285, popularly (and inaccurately) known as the "Pierced Messiah" text. Robert Eisenman and Michael Wise released a statement about the text to the press on November 7, 1991, which prompted startling headlines:

> MESSIANIC LINK TO CHRISTIANITY IS FOUND IN SCROLLS (*New York Times*)
>
> SCROLLS SUGGEST EARLY JEWISH-CHRISTIAN LINK (*Chicago Tribune*)
>
> MESSIAH-LIKE LEADER MENTIONED IN SCROLLS (*Washington Post*)

The text causing this furor was a tiny fragment with very little complete context. In Eisenman and Wise's translation, it runs:

> [. . .] Isaiah the Prophet, [The thickets of the forest] will be fell[ed with an axe and Lebanon shall f]all [by a mighty one]. A staff shall rise from the root of Jesse, [and a Planting from his roots will bear fruit. . . .] the Branch of David. They will enter into judgement with [. . .] and they will put to death the Prince of the Congregation, the Bran[ch of David . . .] and with woundings, and the (high) priest will command . . . [the sl]ai[n of the Kitti[m][13]

Because much of this text is without any complete context to aid in its restoration, almost any interpretation is conjectural.

The phrase that caused the most uproar was "they shall put to death the Prince of the Congregation." This translation is possible. If it is correct, then we would have a case of the Messiah's being killed in battle. The word translated "woundings" could be related to a Hebrew word meaning "to pierce"; this seems to bring the narrative of the text into connection with Christian ideas about the death of the Messiah via the "piercings" of crucifixion. The *Chicago Tribune* even spoke of a "missing link" between Judaism and Christianity.

My impression is that many lay Christians have welcomed this information as somehow confirming Christian beliefs. (Someone at my church told me at the time that the Dead Sea Scrolls "have confirmed Christ's death on the cross.") The Jewish-Christian evangelist Zola Levitt featured this text along with an interview with Michael Wise in his video "Secrets of the Dead Sea Scrolls." Levitt apparently believes that the text confirms a Jewish-Christian origin of the Qumran sect.

It is hard to understand this reaction. Even if Eisenman and Wise's translation is correct, it would refer to the death of the Messiah in battle, not to his crucifixion or atoning self-sacrifice. The "piercings" would have to refer to mutilations inflicted on the prince's corpse. So other than in the common occurrence of a messianic figure's death, we do not have here a true parallel to any distinctively Christian belief.

Virtually all scholars are agreed now that Eisenman and Wise's interpretation is very likely wrong. The phrase "they put to death the Prince of the Congregation" should probably be understood as "the Prince of the Congregation put (or shall put) him [i.e., the enemy leader] to death."[14] Geza Vermes points out that the text seems to be presented as a fulfillment of the messianic prophecy from Isaiah 11:1–5, which contains the phrase "with the breath of his lips he will slay the wicked." The word translated "slay" is the same word translated "put to death" in the fragment. It is more logical to assume that the prince is portrayed as slaying the wicked rather than the other way around.[15]

The reference to "piercings" may refer to indignities inflicted on the enemy's corpse, or, as Martin Abegg suggests, the word, by another etymology, may refer to the "dancing" of celebrants after the victory of the Prince. It may also refer to "profanations" or "pollutions" of the Gentiles that the priest mentioned in the last line would have to cleanse. Obviously that kind of interpretation is more the kind of thing that one would expect in a text about the warlike Prince of the Congregation. Text 4Q285 may be part of the hitherto missing last column of the *War Scroll,* which narrates the victorious end of the last war against the Sons of Darkness.

The fact is that the text is so fragmentary that we may never know what it really was about. Both Eisenman and Wise have backed off from their initial strong statements about the significance of the scroll.[16]

The Anointed Priest

Except for the unique title "Prince of the Congregation," the concept of the Davidic Messiah as a military deliverer presented in the Dead Sea Scrolls falls into line with Judaism as a whole. But the sect also had the uncommon notion that the Messiah in the latter days would be accompanied by an Anointed Priest, in effect, a second Messiah from the tribe of Levi.

The biblical basis for this belief could be found in 1 Samuel 2:35: "I will raise up for myself a faithful priest, who will do according to what is in my heart and mind. I will firmly establish his house, and he will minister before my anointed one always." Here the royal Anointed One/Messiah is associated with the "faithful priest." The prophet Zechariah saw in a vision a golden lampstand flanked by two olive trees, the lampstand representing God, and the two olive trees "the two who are anointed to serve the LORD of all the earth" (Zech. 4:14)—the king and the priest. So the idea of a cooperative rule between king and priest has Old Testament precedents.

This basic notion was already known prior to the Qumran discoveries from the *Damascus Document,* which refers to the "Messiah of Aaron and Israel," whose coming will usher in a "time of retribution" (XIX, 10) and bring an end to the "time of wickedness" (XII, 23). Before the Qumran discoveries, scholars debated whether the "Messiah of Aaron and Israel" was one person or two: the Messiah of Aaron (Priestly Messiah) and the Messiah of Israel (Davidic Messiah). The second interpretation was confirmed when the Dead Sea Scrolls came to light. The *Manual of Discipline* clearly mentions "Messiahs," plural, again in an eschatological context:

> They shall be judged by the ancient precepts . . . until the coming of the Prophet and the Messiahs of Aaron and Israel (IX, 11).

Scholars were quick to observe that a similar concept of two Messiahs, one from Levi/Aaron and one from Judah/Israel, was found in the intertestamental book called *The Testaments of the Twelve Patriarchs,* a collection of "testaments" (in the sense of "last will and testament") attributed, by a literary fiction, to the twelve sons of Jacob. There the children of Israel are commanded to "honor Levi and Judah, because from them shall arise the salvation of Israel" (Testament of Joseph 19:11; Naphtali 8:2).[17] But Levi shall be superior. "To me," says Judah, "God has given the kingship and to him, the priesthood; and he has subjected the kingship to the priesthood" (Testament of Judah 21:2). Indeed, it is from Levi that the Deliverer shall come in the last days.

> The Lord will raise up a new priest . . . [who] will shine forth like the sun in the earth. . . . In his priesthood sin shall cease and lawless men shall rest from their evil deeds, and righteous men shall find rest in him. And he shall open the gates of paradise . . . (Testament of Levi 18:2, 4, 9–10).

The *Testaments,* or an earlier form of some of them, apparently were highly valued by the Qumran sect. It has even been suggested that the Qumranians wrote them, although this is improbable. But the messianic doctrine of both seems to be the same: At the close of the age, a king from David's line and a priest from Aaron's would appear to bring in a new era of God's blessing, and the Priest would have precedence.

This comes out quite plainly in the scroll known as the *Rule of the Congregation*. The *Rule* provides instructions for entry into the sect "in the latter days" and defines the status of each member of the end-time community. In the assembly, the Priest-Messiah shall enter first,[18] as "the head of the whole congregation of Israel"; then the rest of the priests, followed by the Messiah of Israel, and after him the "heads of the clans of Israel" (II, 11–16). At the communal meal of bread and wine that follows,[19] the Priest, as the spiritual leader of the group, was to say the blessing and lead in the taking of the bread.

The excerpt quoted above from the *Testament of Levi* also appears in Text 4Q541, in a different form:

> He shall make atonement for all the children of his generation, and he will be sent to the children of his generation. His command is like the command of heaven, and they will learn it as if it were the will of God. It shall shine as the eternal sun, and its fire will grow hot in all the ends of the earth, and it shall illumine darkness. Then darkness will pass from the earth, and gloom from the land.

This is obviously the same tradition as the *Testament of Levi*'s "new priest" who "will shine forth like the sun in the earth; he shall take away all darkness from under heaven" (18:4). But the Qumran version continues differently. After the words just quoted, the tone changes abruptly:

> They shall speak many words against him, and many lies; and they shall invent falsehoods against him, and speak insults against him. That evil and crooked generation shall be [. . .] His term of office shall be marked by lies and violence; and the people shall go astray in his days.[20]

This addition is exceedingly strange. How can the priest banish darkness from the land and yet have his term of office marked by lies and violence?

I think the answer is found in the Greek *Testament of Levi.* There we read that each "jubilee," or fifty-year period, of Israel's history is to have its own Anointed Priest. The first two jubilees are joyous ones for the Priest who shall hold office; but the third and fourth ones shall be sorrowful. "The fourth priesthood shall be with sufferings, because injustice shall be imposed upon him in a high degree, and all Israel shall hate each one his neighbor" (17:5). It is possible that the Priest of 4Q541 is not the final Anointed Priest, but rather the priest of the fourth jubilee.[21]

It is natural that the Qumran community should prize the role of the Anointed Priest so highly. Whether they were Essenes or Sadducees or anything else, it is clear that they were of priestly origin. Perhaps they believed that the Anointed Priest of the last age would appear among their community.[22]

The Prophet and Other Messianic Figures

In the book of Deuteronomy, Moses speaks of a coming prophet like himself: "The LORD your God will raise up for you a prophet like me from among your own brothers. You must listen to him" (18:15). This "Prophet" in later times was expected to appear at the end of the age. The *Manual of Discipline* mentions the expectation of "the Prophet and the Messiahs of Aaron and Israel" (IX, 11). In the New Testament, John the Baptist was asked if he were the Messiah or the Prophet (John 1:20–21). Jesus was also thought to be the Prophet (John 6:14).

A fragmentary scroll found in Cave 11 also seems to speak of the Prophet as a forerunner of the time of redemption. The text, usually referred to as 11QMelchizedek, seems to be a *pesher* type of commentary. It strings together various biblical verses with commentary to give a comprehensive picture of God's coming redemption of Israel through the intervention of "Melchizedek," who is also, apparently, the archangel Michael, the Prince of Light. Before that intervention (also described in the *War Scroll*), a figure shall come who is described in Isaiah 52:7: one who "brings good news, who proclaims peace, who brings good tidings, who proclaims salvation."

> The "one who brings good news" is the one anointed (*mashiah*) with the spirit [. . .] he shall make them wise in all the eras of wrath.

This "one anointed with the spirit" seems to be the Prophet, or at least a prophet, one who would foretell all that was to come. Interestingly, 4Q375 refers to Moses as "God's anointed."

> Cursed is the man who does not arise and observe and do according to all the commandments of the Lord in the mouth of Moses his Anointed One (*mashiah*), and to walk after the Lord, the God of our fathers, who commands us from Mount Sinai . . . [The people] stood afar off . . . but Moses, the man of God, was with God in the cloud . . . and like an angel he [God] speaks from his mouth. . . .[23]

As far as I know, this is the only Jewish text that speaks of Moses as the Anointed One/Messiah. But if David was the model king, and Aaron the model priest, Moses was the prophet *par excellence*. His intimacy with God and his role in mediating the Law made it natural to see him as the one preeminently anointed by God for service. The above passage is significant because it is clearly a rare *symbolic* use of the term *mashiah*. Moses was never literally anointed, being neither priest nor king. Here "anointed" simply means someone who is in the highest degree close to God and qualified to represent him.

We seem in fact to have three messianic figures: the Prophet, the Priest, and the King, corresponding to their Old Testament models Moses, Aaron, and David respectively. It is hard to tell sometimes which one the Dead Sea Scrolls are talking about when they are talking about the latter days.

Compounding the confusion is the fact that the Qumran sect also believed that the prophets had an anointing from the Holy Spirit, and therefore were "anointed ones," "messiahs," in a weaker sense. So when the scrolls use the expression "anointed ones," it refers to the Old Testament prophets, as in the *Damascus Document:* "God taught them"—the faithful remnant of Israel—"by those anointed with his holy spirit, the seers of truth" (II, 12). The Holy Spirit, in Jewish thought, is preeminently the divine power behind prophecy. We also hear that the apostates of Israel "spoke rebellion against the commandments of God by the hand of Moses and also against the holy Anointed Ones" (V, 21–VI, 1). These "anointed ones" could be either priests or prophets. In the *War Scroll* the writer thanks God that "by the hand of your Anointed Ones, the seers of times, you have declared to us the eras of the wars of your hands" (XI, 8). These "messiahs," too, could be priests or prophets, but probably the latter.

An example of this confusion is in the interpretation of the "new" text 4Q521. This text has been dubbed "The Messiah of Heaven and Earth" by Eisenman and Wise and has been studied in greater depth by Wise and James Tabor.[24] The latter claim that:

> Our Qumran text, 4Q521, is, astonishingly, quite close to this Christian concept of the messiah. . . . [T]he Messiah of our text, 4Q521, controls heaven and earth, heals the wounded and raises the dead. He rules over nature. Even death, that old enemy, cannot stand before him (he will resurrect the dead).[25]

Text 4Q521 can be rendered as Wise and Tabor do it. But in my opinion they have overinterpreted this text. The vital portion is found in the first two lines:

> [. . . The hea]vens and the earth will obey His Messiah, [The sea and all th]at is in them. He will not turn aside from the commandment of the Holy Ones (Wise and Tabor's translation).

"His Messiah" is a possible translation of the Hebrew phrase; so is "his Messiahs," plural. If taken that way, the messiahs could be the Messiahs of Aaron and Israel; or they could be the anointed priests, or the anointed prophets, taken as a group. Wise and Tabor have also overlooked the fact that the first two lines are in parallelism. The second line has to repeat the same thought as the first line. This strengthens the plural interpretation (as does the unambiguous plural "your anointed ones" in another fragment from the same scroll). A better translation therefore might be:

> Heaven and earth will obey his anointed ones,
> Nothing in them[26] will turn aside from the commandment of the holy ones.

If this is correct, then the "he" who acts in the rest of the passage must be God:

> He releases the captives, opens the eyes of the blind, lifts up [. . .] . . . he will heal the slain,[27] and will resurrect the dead, and will announce good news to the humble. . . .[28]

The meaning of the passage seems to be that God's "anointed ones" and "holy ones"—probably the priests—as representatives of all redeemed Israel will be at the center of the new creation in the messianic age, in which God's healing and saving activity will have free rein. The "anointed ones" are not mentioned past the second line of the text.

Wise and Tabor rightly emphasize the connection between 4Q521 and Luke 7:22 (= Matthew 11:5). In the context, John the Baptist has sent a message asking about "the deeds of the Messiah" (Matt. 11:2; "what Christ was doing" in the NIV is less accurate), wondering whether Jesus is "he who was to come" (Luke 7:20). Jesus replies, "The blind receive sight, the lame walk, those who have leprosy are cured, the deaf hear, the dead are raised, and the good news is preached to the poor. Blessed is the man who does not fall away on account of me" (Luke 7:22–23).

John the Baptist, according to this passage, had begun to have second thoughts about Jesus' messiahship. Jesus had not begun to "destroy unrighteous rulers" or to "smite the Gentiles like a potter's vessel." Was he then really the one who was to come? Jesus' response is to point to the clear signs of God's healing and mercy in his own ministry—acts that, according to the Old Testament, were signs of the arrival of God's redemption.

What 4Q521 gives us is a Jewish text from around the time of Jesus that shows what the traits of the age of redemption were thought to be. Since Jesus' words partially match the Dead Sea Scroll text (the last two items are the same),[29] it may be that these characteristics had already developed a fixed form by his time. The fact that 4Q521 assigns the redeeming actions to God instead of to human beings simply verifies that Jesus claimed that God was uniquely present in his own ministry.

The word *Messiah* in the Dead Sea Scrolls is therefore a term whose meaning wavers and fluctuates. If the same was true of Israel in general, then "Messiah" could mean many different things, along with its central meaning of "Davidic deliverer."

"The Son of God" Text

The final "messianic" text to be discussed is one that scholars have already copiously discussed and are sure to write about for years to come. Known as 4Q246, this Aramaic document is informally referred to as "the son of God" text. J. T. Milik acquired the fragment from Kando in 1958. Joseph Fitzmyer published part of it in 1974 based on a portion of the text that Milik had released, and recently the whole text has been published.[30] It consists of two surviving columns. Half of the first one is torn away; the second is intact. My own translation and understanding of the first column of the text reads:

> [. . . upon] him rested and he fell before the throne. [. . .] forever. Wrath is coming, and your years (?) [. . .] your vision. And all of it is coming to [this] age [. . .] tribulation shall come on the land. [. . .] and slaughters. And a leader of nations [shall arise . . .] king of Assyria and Egypt [. . .] he shall be ruler over the land [. . .] and all shall be enslaved and shall serve [. . .] great he shall be called and by his name he shall be designated.

It is hard to tell exactly what is happening here, but it looks as if a seer of some kind, like the biblical Daniel, is interpreting a vision to a king. The vision is one of disaster. Tribulation and war are coming. In this time of tribulation a leader will arise, who will be king of the gentile nations of Assyria and Egypt. He will establish his rule over the land. At the end of the column somebody shall be called by another's name. The first half of the second column reads:

> He will be called the Son of God, and the son of the Most High they shall call him. Like the meteors that you saw, so will be their kingdom. They will reign over the land for a few years, and they will crush everyone. People will crush people, nation will crush nation.

The obvious question is, Who is this "Son of God"? Fitzmyer suggested that he was "a son of some enthroned king, possibly an heir to the Davidic throne"[31]—in other words, the Messiah, although Fitzmyer stresses that that title is not used here. Another Qumran scholar, F. Garcia-Martinez, believes that the Son of God is the archangel Michael.[32] They believe the Son to be a saving figure.

The problem with these views is that the "Son of God" does not bring peace or redemption. He is preceded by tribulation. He is followed by destruction and violence. For this reason Milik originally thought the "Son of God" was one of the Greek kings who oppressed the Jews during the Hasmonean period and who, like many of the gentile kings, claimed to be divine. In Milik's view, the text was history disguised as prophecy. Similarly, the Israeli scholar David Flusser believed the Son to be the anti-Christ, an evil human ruler who demanded worship as a divine being, and whose appearance in the last days would precede the direct intervention of God.[33]

Probably Milik and especially Flusser were closer to the truth than Fitzmyer and Garcia-Martinez. The key is to notice that, after the "Son of God" is introduced, the text goes on to talk about "*their* kingdom." Who are "they"? There must be more than one ruler. Probably the "king of Assyria and Egypt" is the first ruler, and the Son of God, his son or successor, a king who claims divine honors, the second ruler. The fragmentary end of the first column must originally have read like this:

> [His son] shall be called great, and by his name he shall be designated

—that is, the son shall have the same name as his father. But "their kingdom" shall be as brief as a meteor's flash. (The king that the seer is talking to must have seen meteors in his vision.)

The text ends this way:

> Then the people of God shall arise, and all will have rest from the sword. Their[34] kingdom is an eternal kingdom, and all their ways are in truth. They shall judge the land in truth, and all will make peace. The sword will cease from the land, and all the nations will bow down to them. The great God is his strength; he himself will fight for them. He will put the nations in their power, and all of them he will place before them. His [or *their*] dominion is an eternal dominion, and all the deeps [*fragment ends*].

Text 4Q246 may be, as Milik thinks, history disguised as prophecy. It tells of the victory of the people of God over evil rulers. The Son of God may be the archvillain Antiochus IV Epiphanes, who claimed to be the manifestation on earth of Zeus, and who, trying to stamp out the Jewish religion, ignited the Maccabean revolution in 167 B.C. ("the people of God shall arise").

In any case, this text is too ambiguous to be available to enlighten us about messianic interpretation at Qumran. Fitzmyer stressed the similarity of the expressions to Luke 1:32–33, in the annunciation to Mary: "He [Jesus] will be great and will be called the Son of the Most High. The Lord God will give him the throne of his father David, and he will reign over the house of Jacob forever; his kingdom will never end." Are these passages related and, if so, how? If the "Son of God" text refers to the Messiah, then the gospel might have been suggesting that Jesus was the fulfillment of what was then a famous, though uncanonical, prophecy.

But, as we have seen, 4Q246 probably does not refer to a Messiah, or even to a good person. Though the Qumran text and the Luke passage have some expressions in common, the latter speaks about Jesus' birth as a fulfillment of the promise made to David's descendant: "I will be his father, and he will be my son" (2 Sam. 7:14). In 4Q246 there is no trace of the Davidic connection, and the appearance of the "Son of the Most High" is the occasion for suffering, not joy. Therefore it is unlikely that there is any direct connection between these texts.

Christology and the Dead Sea Scrolls

How can the messianic concepts of the scrolls help us better understand the background of the New Testament? Their help is genuine, but limited. They show that some Jews of the first century held views about the Messiah that might have predisposed them to misunderstand the ministry of someone like Jesus, with a different concept of Messiah.

The sect's concept of the Davidic Messiah was not unlike the one held by the rest of Judaism. The sect could not simply mold the messianic hope to fit their own purposes. The messianic expectation had to some extent a given form that the scroll writers simply had to accept, including the Messiah's Davidic descent, his future kingship, his title "Messiah," and his appointed task of "destroying unrighteous rulers." They used the same Old Testament prooftexts as did later Judaism and early Christianity.

Jesus fulfilled the messianic role in a different way. He accepted the title of "Messiah" privately (Matt. 16:13–20) and publicly (Mark 14:61–62). But he rejected the element of messianism that saw armed rebellion and vengeance against gentile despots as a necessary ingredient. Therefore he had to deemphasize the title "Messiah." Although the New Testament stresses Jesus' Davidic descent, Jesus himself emphasized that the work of the Messiah was not simply a repeat of David's military career. The Messiah is David's Lord and so exceeds the boundaries of the conventional ideas of the Messiah (Mark 12:35–37). Jesus as Messiah brought the kingdom of God near for those who became his disciples. The Qumran reference to Moses as "God's Messiah" may show that a mediator between God and Israel could use the title in a looser sense, without the militaristic baggage of the times.

A negative result from the Dead Sea Scrolls is that they do not use the title "son of man" to refer to any messianic-eschatological figure. Jesus' favorite name for himself was "son of man." It was based on the mysterious "one like a son of man" mentioned in Daniel 7:13, a supernatural being who "was given authority, glory and sovereign power" (Dan. 7:14). But the "son of man" is also the meek and lowly One who, like all humanity, is "lower than the heavenly beings" (Pss. 8:4–5; 144:3). This title, then, is peculiarly well-suited to express exaltation and humiliation simultaneously. Scholars have long argued whether Jesus was using an expression whose eschatological meaning was already common in Judaism or whether he gave it that meaning. The Dead Sea Scrolls do not help to decide one way or the other. All we know is that none of their important messianic figures were called "son of man."

The Priestly Messiah has some similarities to New Testament concepts. Jesus is portrayed as a High Priest in the letter to the Hebrews (e.g., 5:1–6). Jesus, not being of Levi, could not have been seen as the Priest of the end time, but, like the Priest, his utterance was "like the command of heaven," and "many spoke insults against him," as in the scroll 4Q541. But most of the central Qumran notions connected to the Messiah of Aaron are absent from the New Testament.

Another negative result is that the scrolls do not call the Messiah the "son of God." Although the prophecy in 2 Samuel 7:14 ("he will be my son") is applied to the Branch of David in the

Florilegium, the prophecy does not generate a durable title, like "Branch of David" or "Prince of the Congregation." In writings from other branches of Judaism, particularly righteous men could be called "God's son,"[35] and the angels were sometimes known in the Old Testament as "sons of God." God was said to have "begotten" the King (Ps. 2:7, KJV, NRSV), especially of the seed of David (2 Sam. 7:14). Israel as a nation was God's firstborn son (Ex. 4:22). Therefore, as one scholar concludes, "there was nothing particularly unique about calling someone 'son of God' at the time of Jesus."[36] Then why did Jews react negatively to Jesus' use of the term?

Qumran can help us here. It is true that in this period someone by virtue of his royal office or great piety, might, in a moment of high exaltation, be recognized as specially favored by God, and accordingly called God's "son." But that momentary acclamation never becomes a fixed title or intrinsic name of the person so complimented. "The son of God" never becomes merely a synonym for the Messiah or the man of God. It is always used sparingly and figuratively. In fact, apart from 4Q246, no one, including the Teacher of Righteousness, is described by this title. Although God may be addressed as "Father" in the psalms of the sect, no member of the sect is called his son.

Indeed, 4Q246 shows us how blasphemous the *title* Son of God was thought to be. It clearly implies that part of the gentile ruler's wickedness was in claiming that designation as a fixed prerogative. Although someone could be called "a" son of God, no one could be "the" son of God. (The Aramaic phrase must be translated "the," not "a," Son of God.) The Qumran writer evidently saw this claim as an assertion of equality with God.

All of this throws light on the use of the term "Son of God" in the New Testament. According to John 3:16, Jesus is God's "only Son." Jesus' continual reference to himself as "the Son" prompted his opponents to accuse him of blasphemy (John 10:33, 36). The high priest's question in Mark 14:61, "Are you the Christ, the son of the Blessed One?" makes sense against this background. He did not mean, "Are you claiming to be the Messiah, by royal status a son of God?" He meant, "Are you that messianic claimant who is reputed to call himself 'the' Son of God?" When Jesus responded, "I am," the priest considered this to be blasphemy worthy of death

(Mark 14:64). Claiming to be the Messiah was not blasphemy. Claiming to be *the* Son of God was. Text 4Q246, in its negative portrayal of "the Son of God," typifies the mindset behind that attitude.

Finally, the Qumran expectation of "the Prophet" falls into line with the general Jewish expectation of the successor to Moses. The Qumranians do not much emphasize this forerunner of the royal Messiah, unless the "Interpreter of the Law" or the Teacher of Righteousness himself were considered to be the Prophet. It is more likely that those figures, in their inspired interpretations of Scripture, were thought to pave the way for the coming of the ideal Prophet, Priest, and King.

Jesus was considered to be a prophet (Luke 7:16; John 6:14). Sometimes he allowed this title to be applied to him (Luke 7:16; 24:19), but in general he did not encourage it. It was too narrow a basis for understanding his life and work.

In comparing Qumran messiology and the New Testament's Christology, we can see that Jesus' mission was bigger than any one messianic concept. He accepted popular designations of Messiah and Prophet, but he favored more inclusive, less common, and even difficult, concepts like "Son of Man," "Son of God," and "Servant of the Lord" to hint at his true nature, paving the way for his followers to hail him as Lord after his resurrection. Thereafter, all the messianic designations and categories are seen to converge on him. Such a focus on the claims of one actual individual, who partakes of the usual categories in unexpected ways, but who validates them by his life and mission, is wholly unlike the hope expressed in the Dead Sea Scrolls.

The scrolls, then, help us fill in the picture of the beliefs of first-century Judaism. By and large, they confirm the impressions already gained from other sources, but they add vivid details and suggest further lines of research. Some of the texts with messianic significance are obscure and may require years of scholarly discussion before they can make their proper contribution to our knowledge. Most of all, the scrolls bring to the reader, with unprecedented richness, the hopes and expectations of a group of faithful Jews.

For they did have hopes in abundance. Messianism was not the center of this sect's faith. Obedience to the Law as they conceived it was. But they looked forward to God's redemption of Israel as ardently as they looked backward to his past mercies. As Christians, we may hope and believe that God, having seen that "they sought Him with a whole heart" (*Damascus Document* I, 10), allowed some of them to perceive the true fulfillment of their yearnings in the ministry of Jesus of Nazareth.

Notes

1. Three significant books have recently been reprinted: *The Scrolls and the New Testament,* ed. Krister Stendahl (1957; reprint, New York: Crossroad, 1992); *John and the Dead Sea Scrolls,* ed. James H. Charlesworth (New York: Crossroad, 1991); and *Paul and the Dead Sea Scrolls,* ed. Jerome Murphy-O'Connor (New York: Crossroad, 1991). Also highly recommended is William Sanford LaSor, *The Dead Sea Scrolls and the New Testament* (Grand Rapids: Eerdmans, 1972).

2. An excellent entry into the whole spectrum of ancient writings important for understanding the New Testament is Craig A. Evans's *Noncanonical Writings and New Testament Interpretation* (Peabody, Mass.: Hendrickson, 1992).

3. The Mishnah, dating from around A.D. 200, is a collection of Jewish religous laws. It forms the central document of the larger collection of laws and tales known as the Talmud.

4. Milik, *Ten Years of Discovery,* 130.

5. Joseph Fitzmyer, "The Languages of Palestine in the First Century A.D.," in *A Wandering Aramean: Collected Aramaic Essays* (Missoula, Mont.: Scholars Press, 1979), 46.

6. Randall Buth, "Hebrew Poetic Tenses and the Magnificat," *Journal for the Study of the New Testament* 21 (1984): 67–83.

7. Edgar Goodspeed, "The Original Language of the Gospels," in *Contemporary Thinking About Jesus: An Anthology,* ed. Thomas S. Kepler (New York: Abingdon-Cokesbury, 1944), 59. The original article appeared in 1934.

8. The mention of the "Anointed One, the ruler" in Daniel 9:25 might be the one exception. To me, however, this passage is too obscure to cast any light on ideas of the Messiah.

9. Quoted from R. B. Wright, "Psalms of Solomon," in James H. Charlesworth, ed., *The Old Testament Pseudepigrapha,* vol. 2 (New York: Doubleday, 1985), 667. The Psalms were originally written in Hebrew, but survive only in Greek translation.

10. A list, with discussion of each, can be found in Evans, *Noncanonical Writings,* 242–52. Josephus does not use the term "Messiah."

11. The Palestinian Targum according to Codex Neofiti, Genesis 49:11. Although this text comes from post-Christian times, it probably represents concepts in vogue from the pre-Christian era.

12. Targum Onkelos on Genesis 49:11.

13. Eisenman and Wise, *The Dead Sea Scrolls Uncovered,* 29. Their text actually reads "Leader of the Community" instead of "Prince of the Congregation."

14. Those who do not know Hebrew may well wonder that intelligent people can differ so widely on such a fundamental point as the tense and person of a verb. Briefly, because Hebrew is usually written without vowels, context is far more important for the proper understanding of a Hebrew text than for an English text. In fragmentary texts, the possibilities for ambiguity are numerous. In this text, the word transliterated WHMYTW can mean, in the absence of further context, "and they shall kill" or "and he shall kill him" or the past forms of either phrase: "and they killed" or "and he killed him."

15. Geza Vermes, "The 'Pierced Messiah' Text—An Interpretation Evaporates," *Biblical Archaeology Review* (July/August 1992): 80–82. James Tabor responded to Vermes in "A Pierced or Piercing Messiah?—The Verdict Is Still Out," *BAR* (November/December 1993): 58–59.

16. Eisenman attributes the interpretation to Wise: "I *never* said there was a concept of a 'suffering Messiah' at Qumran. . . . To be precise, this interpretation . . . was originally Professor Wise's." Yet Eisenman was the member of the duo who released the statement to the press. Why? Eisenman says his motives were "to gainsay the notion that there was nothing interesting in the unpublished corpus" and "to show that the links between early Christianity and Qumran were much closer than previously thought" (*Biblical Archaeology Review* [January/February 1993]: 66). Without a "suffering Messiah," however, Eisenman cannot show "much closer" links between the scrolls and Christianity than he has shown elsewhere. As for the first motive, one may question whether a scholar should go to the press with a "discovery" that he himself does not believe in.

17. All quotations are from H. C. Kee, "Testaments of the Twelve Patriarchs," in James Charlesworth, ed., *The Old Testament Pseudepigrapha,* vol. 1 (New York: Doubleday, 1983), 775–828.

18. The line of text describing the entrance of the Priest-Messiah is fragmentary and has been restored in different ways, some controversial. D. Barthélemy restored the text as "when [God] shall b[eg]et the Messiah with them." The word *God* is wholly restored, *beget* partially so. Predictably this led to all kinds of statements about God's begetting of the Messiah as a parallel to New Testament doctrine. The context, however, encourages the restoration "the Anointed [Priest] (or Priest-Messiah) shall [come] with them, [for he is] the head of the whole Congregation." See K. G. Kuhn, "The Two Messiahs of Aaron and Israel," in Stendahl, *The Scrolls and the New Testament,* 56.

19. The mere mention of "bread and wine" caused some popular writers to lose all perspective and to start talking about the resemblance between Christian Communion and the communal meal of the Essenes. A. Powell Davies, for instance, wrote, "It seems altogether likely . . . that the bread represented the Messiahs of Aaron and Israel in the sacramental meal of the Qumran covenanters. . . . [The wine] was the blood . . . of the

Messiahs. Through the bread that was flesh and the wine that was blood the Messiahs were present with their people. . . . This, then, was the Essenic sacred meal, so close as to be almost identical with the sacred meal of the early Christians" (*The Meaning of the Dead Sea Scrolls* [New York: New American Library, 1956], 100–101). Bread and wine were elements in almost every meal consumed in ancient Palestine; that is why Jesus chose them as the media through which his own atoning sacrifice was to be commemorated. There is nothing in the Qumran texts about the bread and wine being the body and blood of any Messiah, nor does the meal commemorate a saving sacrifice. They drank wine and ate bread. So did (and do) Christians, and there the resemblance ends.

20. This text, 4Q541, is found in Emile Puech, "Fragments d'un apocryphe de Lévi et le personnage eschatologique, 4QTestLévi(?) et 4QAJa," *Madrid Qumran Congress: Proceedings of the International Congress on the Dead Sea Scrolls, Madrid, 18–21 March 1991,* ed. J. Trebolle Barrera and L. Vegas Montaner (Leiden: Brill, 1992), 449–529; and in Eisenman and Wise, *The Dead Sea Scrolls Uncovered,* 142–45. My translation and readings differ somewhat from both sources.

21. The text 4Q375 emphasizes that the truest anointing is that of the Priest:

> All that your God commands you from the mouth of the prophet you shall observe. . . . But the prophet who shall arise and speak rebellion to you, to turn you away from your God, shall be put to death. And if the tribe that he [the prophet] is from shall arise and say, "He shall not be put to death! He is a righteous man, and a faithful prophet!"—then come with that tribe and your elders and your judges . . . before the Anointed (*ha-mashiah*) Priest, on whose head has been poured the oil of anointing.

This does not seem to be an eschatological text, however, and therefore should not be considered "messianic."

22. This raises the interesting question of whether the Qumran sect believed the Teacher of Righteousness was the Priestly Messiah. Although he is called a priest, he is never referred to as "anointed" (*mashiah*), nor are any of the usual messianic prooftexts from the Old Testament applied to him. Nevertheless, some have suggested that the Teacher of Righteousness was the same as the "Interpreter of the Law" mentioned with the Branch of David in the *Florilegium* quoted previously (p. 160); and in the *Damascus Document,* the "Interpreter" is also paired with the Prince of the Congregation (VII,18). In those texts, the "Interpreter" could be the same as the Priestly Messiah, or he could be the "Prophet like Moses."

Earlier in the *Damascus Document* the Interpreter seems to be a figure from the past who founded the sect, establishing laws for them to walk in "until the appearance of the one who shall teach righteousness in the latter days" (VI,10–11). There the Interpreter seems to be different from the Teacher, who seems to be the still-expected figure. In other words, the Interpreter and the Teacher seem to have switched places. There doesn't seem to be any way to shuffle these texts to produce a consistent result. The sect may have attached different titles to the same figures, or have associated the same name with different people.

23. John Strugnell, "Moses-Pseudepigrapha at Qumran: 4Q375, 4Q376, and Similar Works," in L. Schiffman, ed., *Archaeology and History in the Dead Sea Scrolls* (Sheffield: JSOT Press, 1990), 221–56.

24. Eisenman and Wise, *The Dead Sea Scrolls Uncovered,* 19–23; Wise and James Tabor, "The Messiah at Qumran," *Biblical Archaeology Review* (November/December 1992): 60–65.

25. Wise and Tabor, "The Messiah at Qumran," 60–61.

26. Wise and Tabor restore "the sea and all. . . ." There is not enough room in the text for the letters required for this restoration.

27. Wise and Tabor's "heal the sick" is incorrect; the Hebrew word means "slain."

28. In line 11, immediately preceding this excerpt, Wise and Tabor translate "as for the wonders that are not the work of the Lord, when he (i.e., the Messiah) [comes]. . . ." This line is difficult, but probably is not as Wise and Tabor understand it. I propose "as for wonders that never were, (they are) the work of the Lord," followed by the excerpt just quoted.

29. The mention of "healing the slain (or corpses)" is absent in Jesus' formulation of the time of salvation. It is possible that 4Q521, in a section now lost, had some kind of narrative about the last war against the unrighteous. After the war, God would raise up the warriors of Israel who had fallen.

30. Fitzmyer's original publication was in "The Contribution of Qumran Aramaic to the Study of the New Testament," *New Testament Studies* 20 (1973–74): 391–94. The complete publication is Emile Puech, "Fragment d'une apocalypse en araméen (4Q246 = pseudo-Dan^{d}) et le 'royaume de Dieu'" (Fragment of an Apocalypse in Aramaic [4Q246 = pseudo-Dan^{d}] and the "Kingdom of God"), *Revue Biblique* 99 (1992): 98–131.

31. Fitzmyer, *A Wandering Aramean,* 106. See also John Collins, "A Pre-Christian 'Son of God' Among the Dead Sea Scrolls," *Bible Review* 9 (June 1993): 34–38.

32. F. Garcia-Martinez, *Qumran and Apocalyptic: Studies on the Aramaic Texts From Qumran* (Leiden: Brill, 1992), 173.

33. David Flusser, "The Hubris of the Antichrist in a Fragment from Qumran," *Immanuel* 10 (1980): 31–37.

34. I use "their" here and throughout the quote to indicate that the antecedent is "people." In Aramaic the pronoun is singular, "its/his," because "people" is a masculine singular noun in Aramaic. Those who follow the "messianic" interpretation understand the pronouns to refer to the "Son of God."

35. See the references given in Martin Hengel, *The Son of God: The Origin of Christology and the History of Jewish-Hellenistic Religion,* trans. John Bowden (Philadelphia: Fortress, 1976).

36. James D. G. Dunn, *The Evidence for Jesus* (Philadelphia: Westminster, 1985), 49.

Conclusion

The Mysteries of the Scrolls

Readers may have noticed that almost every theory made about the Qumran sect has to be hedged about with qualifications. If they are Essenes, they are not standard-issue Essenes, but something different. Perhaps they are just "Essenic." If they are Pharisees, they are early Pharisees or extreme Pharisees. If they are Sadducees, they must be breakaway Sadducees. If they were Zealots, they were unusually monkish and scholarly Zealots. If they were Christians, they were heretics (or else every *other* Christian group was heretical). Perhaps they were some little-known or altogether unknown group.

In short, this group and their literature don't quite fit into any of the preexisting slots that history has bestowed on us. Historians have dealt with this fact in different ways. Some (not many) have taken the tack of denying the dependability of the non-Qumran evidence. "Josephus was a liar, or, at least, didn't know what he was talking about. The New Testament is undependable. Philo made it all up." One scholar went so far as to suggest that there never were any Essenes; the passages in Josephus seeming to deal with this group are actually later Christian interpolations. This angle has a certain appeal. Our other sources are second-hand accounts, in a sense, while the scrolls are first-hand evidence.

But first-hand evidence for what? The scrolls are so relentlessly religious, so unceasingly literary, that they seem to construct a smooth inner world of their own, without historical bumps and edges that might locate it in the universe of the past. As we saw in the previous chapter, the help they can give is general and indirect, not specific and direct. We know approximately when the scrolls were written, and where; but even the archaeological and other evidence bearing on their date, as we have seen, is being reconsidered. At the moment, the scrolls seem to be floating untethered over the landscape of Israel's history.

That is an exaggeration, of course, but not much of one. Shemaryahu Talmon, a long-time Israeli specialist in Qumran studies and a member of the Scroll Oversight Committee, has written:

> The writings which emanate from the Qumran caves were evidently produced by Jewish authors who lived in the last centuries before and the first century after the turn of the era. These documents thus contain contemporaneous, first-hand evidence which relates directly to this crucial period. One could expect with much justification that they would enlighten us on that "dark age" in the history of Judaism.
>
> These great hopes did not materialize. The most painstaking analysis of the Qumran documents has not shed new light on historical events which affected Judaism as a whole in those times, nor on significant developments which then occurred in Jewish concepts and beliefs. Moreover there remains much uncertainty even in regard to matters which pertain specifically, in fact exclusively, to the Qumran Covenanters themselves: *inter alia,* the genesis, history, and societal structure of their community, their particular theology and ritual code.[1]

Nothing could have been more unexpected than this result: that first-hand documents stemming from the second century B.C. to the first century A.D. should have contributed so much less than expected to our knowledge of that time period. Is this in fact the case? Are we still, in terms of our knowledge of antiquity, right where we were 1947? Literary critic Robert Alter, like Talmon, also believes that the discovery of the Dead Sea Scrolls promised much but delivered little:

> The popular fascination with the scrolls that has been sustained for over four decades and the inordinate hopes for a grand revelation from these scraps of parchment betoken one of the great modern illusions—that if only we could take within our grasp the material substance of the past, if only we could empty out all the contents of its buried time capsules, we might touch an ultimate secret of origins, understand in a new and illuminating way how we came to be what we are. Whatever the wealth of historical testimony discovered in the Qumran texts, and perhaps still to be discovered, we will almost certainly not find in them any such truth of origins.[2]

Alter put his finger on one of the key reasons for popular interest in the scrolls. Illuminating the past is one way of illuminating the present. People expected validation for their own beliefs (or unbeliefs) to emerge from the caves. It may be true, as Hershel Shanks has written, "these tatters will tell us where we came from,"[3] but so far the scrolls have disappointed this expectation.

But it is possible to overstate the "unimportance" of the scrolls, as Alter and Talmon arguably have done. Although the impact of the scrolls falls short of a revolution, it is undeniable that in certain areas they have effected a renaissance. There is no room in this book to spell out all the scrolls have meant for the textual criticism of the Old Testament and the formation of the Hebrew canon of Scripture; suffice it to say that those fields of study will never be the same.[4] I hope a reading of this book will also show how they can enrich our understanding of the New Testament world.

But perhaps the greatest gift the scrolls have given us is simply to enlarge our sense of the complexity and variety of history. In some ways, the past is as uncertain as the future, and almost as little known. Perhaps we shall have to be content with that lesson, at least until the next time ancient manuscripts emerge from their hiding places to delight, bewilder, and challenge us.

Notes

1. S. Talmon, "Between the Bible and the Mishnah: Qumran from Within," *Jewish Civilization in the Hellenistic-Roman Period* (Philadelphia: Trinity Press, 1991), 219–20.
2. Robert Alter, "How Important Are the Dead Sea Scrolls?" *Commentary* 92 (February 1992): 41.

3. Publisher's foreword, *A Fascimile Edition of the Dead Sea Scrolls*, vol. 1, prepared with an introduction and index by Robert H. Eisenman and James M. Robinson (Washington, D.C.: Biblical Archaeology Society, 1991), xii.

4. See the appendix for a discussion of these specialized topics.

Appendix

The Old Testament in Light of the Scrolls

The discovery of the Dead Sea Scrolls has probably made its greatest impact in the study of the Hebrew text of the Old Testament. I have already described the elation the early discoverers felt when they identified the complete Isaiah scroll from Cave 1 as the oldest known manuscript of an Old Testament book. That scroll, as well as the fragmentary Isaiah scroll from the same cave, corroborated the antiquity of the traditional Jewish Bible known as the Masoretic text.

That was nice to know, but it was not earth-shattering. Much more significant was Frank Cross's discovery in the early fifties of a copy of 1 Samuel that confirmed the antiquity of the Hebrew text that was the basis of the Septuagint.

The Septuagint is the oldest of all Bible translations and has helped students of the Old Testament throughout history to understand some difficult sections of the biblical text, since, for most books, the Septuagint reproduces in Greek substantially the same Old Testament that is found in the Hebrew Masoretic text. Despite the overall agreement between the Septuagint and the Masoretic text, however, there are numerous differences that range from small matters of, say, the tense and number of verbal forms or the choice of vocabulary to variations in the order of chapters. In some cases, the Septuagint has verses or paragraphs not found in the Masoretic text. These differences have caused the Septuagint to play a fluctuating role in Old Testament textual criticism. Some scholars said that the differences were due to the translators and not to the underlying text, and therefore the differences could be ignored. Others believed that the Greek translators had actually used as their basis a Hebrew Old Testament somewhat different from the Masoretic text.

Cross's discovery settled the question in favor of the second group of scholars. He identified several fragments of scroll as the opening chapters of 1 Samuel. The scroll, called 4QSam[a], agreed in several important respects with the Septuagint where it differed from the Masoretic text. For instance, the Septuagint adds an extra line to these from the "Song of Hannah" (1 Sam. 2:8):

> He raises the poor from the dust
> and lifts the needy from the ash heap;
> he seats them with princes
> and has them inherit a throne of honor.

The Septuagint adds:

> He grants the vow of the one who vows,
> and he blesses the years of the righteous.

Previously, scholars thought that the Septuagint translators added the extra lines to make the song reflect Hannah's situation. But 4QSam[a] had the original Hebrew text of the addition. Other Septuagint variations were also reflected in the scroll.

Now 4QSam[a] was not the only scroll providing proof of the antiquity of the Hebrew text underlying the Septuagint. Cross soon identified another Samuel text, 4QSam[b], that also had similarities to the Septuagint. Patrick Skehan found texts agreeing with the ancient Greek version, such as the Deuteronomy text 4QDeut[q], containing a variant version of the "Song of Moses" from Deuteronomy 32. Others have since been identified.

But Skehan also recognized some Cave 4 scrolls that agreed with the ancient Hebrew text known as the Samaritan Pentateuch. The Samaritans, an ancient Jewish sect that may stem from the same period as the Qumran sect, had (and have—a few hundred Samaritans still survive) their own text of the Pentateuch, differing in many details from the Masoretic text. Before Qumran, most scholars believed that this text was strictly a Samaritan product from later times, since a few of the textual differences involved points of doctrine wherein the Samaritans differed from mainstream Judaism. Skehan's discovery showed that texts like the Samaritan Pentateuch—such as 4QpaleoExod^{m1}—were circulating at the same time as texts resembling the Masoretic and Septuagint texts.

In short, the Dead Sea Scrolls had not only corroborated the antiquity of the Masoretic text, but also of the other main versions of the Old Testament! The fact that three different varieties of Old Testament text were in use at the same time and in the same place begged for an explanation.

Cross argued that each of the three types represented the slightly different Old Testament text used by Jews in three different localities.[2] Egyptian Jews used the Hebrew text that became the basis for the Septuagint translation. The original home of the Masoretic text was Babylon. The Samaritan text was native to Palestine. All of them descended in some way from the original Hebrew text and developed different forms in the course of copying.

Cross's theory has had only limited success. Most scholars preferred to speak simply of the variety of texts as pointing to the "textual fluidity" before the Masoretic text was established as *the* Old Testament text of Judaism. Recently, Emanuel Tov has gone even further. He believes that scholars like Cross saw three "text-types" among the scrolls because they were already familiar with the three "species" of Old Testament (Masoretic, Septuagint, Samaritan). In fact, the affinities of the Qumran Old Testament texts are rarely so clear-cut.

Tov also pointed out that there are plenty of variations in the Qumran scrolls that are not found in any of the Big Three versions. One example is a paragraph in 4QSam^{a}. First Samuel 11 relates how King Saul rescued the city of Jabesh Gilead from Nahash, king of the Ammonites, who had threatened to gouge out the right eye of all the inhabitants. The war with Nahash has always seemed to be curiously sudden and without context. But 4QSam^{a} contains the following paragraph before 1 Samuel 11:

> Now Nahash, king of the Ammonites, had been grievously oppressing the Gadites and the Reubenites. He would gouge out the right

> eye of each of them and would not grant Israel a deliverer. No one was left of the Israelites across the Jordan whose right eye Nahash, king of the Ammonites, had not gouged out. But there were seven thousand men who had escaped from the Ammonites and had entered Jabesh Gilead.

Currently the New Revised Standard Version is the only English version with the Qumran reading.[3] If it is part of the original text of 1 Samuel—and most textual critics today think it is—then it explains the abrupt beginning of the siege of Jabesh Gilead as the last stage of an ongoing war.

The "Nahash paragraph" is the most spectacular example of textual readings unique to the scrolls. Most of the unique Qumran readings are of much less importance. But that there are forms of the text that are unique to the scrolls tells Tov that the Big Three have no monopoly on the Old Testament.

Tov theorizes that instead of three main types of Old Testament text, there were in theory an unlimited number, all of them more or less different from each other. The Big Three survived to our day by sheer happenstance.[4]

The jury is still out on Tov's speculations, but they are not likely to go over any better than Cross's. Tov must admit that the vast majority of Qumran Old Testament texts are palpably aligned with one or the other of the Big Three. His list demonstrates this agreement:

Texts aligned with Masoretic text	: 60 percent.
" " " Samaritan "	: 5 "
" " " Septuagint "	: 5 "
Nonaligned texts	: 10 "
Texts written in Qumran practice	: 20 "[5]

Tov's last two categories are open to question. By "nonaligned" texts he means those that do not clearly line up with any of the Big Three texts. A better word for these would be "mixed" texts, that is, texts that seem to incorporate readings from several traditions. The last category, texts written in "Qumran practice," includes texts—like the intact Isaiah scroll from Cave 1—that Tov considers to have been written in the peculiar spelling and grammar in use at Qumran. But it is surely illegitimate to change the criteria of alignment from *textual* agreement to *grammatical* agreement. The

Isaiah scroll, as we have seen, actually belongs to the Masoretic group. Others in this category belong to the Samaritan (4QNum[b]) or to the mixed (4QSam[c]) group.

The Masoretic family dominates among the Qumran Scrolls. (It is the only type of text found at Masada and the Wadi Murabba'at.) The Old Testament texts were not as unstable in this period as some scholars suppose; the Masoretic text was already beginning to eliminate its rivals. It is possible that the Masoretic group had always enjoyed a certain prestige in Judaism. In that case there would always have been a limit to textual differences.

Of course, all this talk about different kinds of Old Testament texts and missing paragraphs raises a mild theological problem for some Christians. If this kind of variation in the biblical text is so ancient and so common, what becomes of the conviction that the Bible, by God's "singular care and providence" has been "kept pure in all ages" (*Westminster Confession,* I.viii)? If by "pure" one means that the text has been kept pristine and changeless through centuries of copying ever since it left the hands of the original authors, then that doctrine must be discarded.

However, I doubt that anyone but the most ultra-conservative person would make such a claim. Biblical scholars have always been aware of the differences between texts; indeed, in the New Testament one can observe Old Testament quotations that sometimes agree with the Masoretic text, sometimes with the Septuagint, sometimes with neither. The textual footnotes of modern translations like the New International Version provide most of the major variations from the Masoretic text. Attentive readers see that no truly weighty matters are at stake.

The diversity of biblical texts, now reemphasized by the Qumran texts, does not impair "the heavenliness of the matter, the efficacy of the doctrine, the majesty of the style, the consent of all the parts, the scope of the whole" or "the full discovery it makes of the only way of man's salvation" (*Westminster Confession,* I.v). Evangelicals in particular should welcome the help the Dead Sea Scrolls give scholars in reconstructing the original Old Testament text.

The positive achievements of the Qumran discovery for this area of study, then, are three: the confirmation of a true Hebrew text underlying the Septuagint, sanctioning the wider use of that translation in textual criticism; the verification of the antiquity of the Masoretic text; and the suggestion of a greater tolerance for diversity between texts than later became the case.

Qumran and the Old Testament Canon

The Qumran biblical texts have also raised a fourth issue, without casting much light on it: Which books did the Qumran sect consider part of the canon of Scripture? This question is important in some scholars' eyes because the canon of Old Testament Scripture is generally thought to have been closed around the time the Qumran sect came to an end, that is, in the second half of the first century A.D. If we can figure out which books the Qumranians considered to be Scripture, it might clarify the process whereby the Old Testament books were canonized for Judaism as a whole.

So goes the argument. In fact, almost everything about the Qumran "canon" is uncertain. We have no sure way of knowing what books they considered canonical; the caves contain no list of "approved" books. All the scrolls were written on the same material, with the same ink, in the same languages. No doubt the Torah was considered Scripture *par excellence,* as it was in the rest of Judaism. The prophetical books were probably considered inspired, since they were provided with commentary, as were some of the Psalms. And the Qumran literature as a whole shows in almost every line the influence of the canonical (by our standards) Old Testament.

But other books that we consider extracanonical, like the *Book of Jubilees* or the *Book of Enoch,* were also influential at Qumran. They may have considered them divinely inspired. But we have no information on the Qumran criteria for canonicity. We do not know if they had any such criteria. They may have had some kind of in-between category for "authoritative, but noncanonical" works. Even if we knew what the Qumran canon was, we could never be sure if their standards had any relation to those of the rest of Judaism.

Only two bits of evidence from the scrolls may relieve this gloomy conclusion. One is the presence among the Dead Sea Scrolls of what seems to be part of the book of Psalms. The *Psalms Scroll* from Cave 11 contains 41 psalms. Most of them are identical with psalms of the Masoretic text (although given in a different order), but eight of them were previously unknown or known only from ancient translations. Sanders suggests that this scroll—and other fragmentary collections like it from Cave 4—is a remnant of a psalter that is older and longer than our "short" psalter of 150 psalms.[6] That would imply a certain arbitrariness in the selection of psalms for the psalter and would suggest that the book of Psalms did not exist in a fixed form and order until the first century A.D.: The canonization process had not yet reached the book of Psalms.

Two considerations discourage this conclusion. First, a prose insert in the *Psalms Scroll* alludes to the 364-day sectarian calendar, implying that the Qumran psalter was specifically a psalter of the Qumran sect, not a "mainstream" psalter. In other words, the sectarians may have had an alternative book of Psalms. That is interesting, but it does not tell us much about what anyone else's psalter looked like or how far the canonization process had reached for the rest of Israel. Second, not everyone agrees that the *Psalms Scroll* was actually a Psalms scroll; some believe that it may have been a collection of hymns for worship. If so, the *Psalms Scroll* would have no bearing on the question of canon.

Another bit of evidence bearing on the question of canon is a line from 4QMMT that refers to "the book of Moses, and the words of the prophets and David" (C 10), apparently meaning all the books counted as holy writ. Almost the same expression with the same meaning appears in Luke 24:44, "the Law of Moses, the Prophets and the Psalms." This threefold division of the Old Testament is still current in Hebrew Bibles as the *Law,* the *Prophets,* and the *Writings.*[7] The third division was earlier called "Psalms" or "David" because the psalter is usually the first book appearing in it. Previously, the earliest reference to this threefold division was found in the Greek preface to the apocryphal book of Ecclesiasticus: "the Law, the Prophets and the other volumes of the fathers . . . the Law, the Prophets, and the other books." If 4QMMT is dated earlier than the Greek translation of Ecclesiasticus (132 B.C.), as it may well be, then it becomes the first reference we have to the threefold division of the canon. Unfortunately, it tells us nothing about which books were contained in each division.

Notes

1. See Patrick W. Skehan, "Exodus in the Samaritan Recension from Qumran," *Journal of Biblical Literature* 74 (1955): 182–87; and J. E.

Sanderson, *An Exodus Scroll From Qumran* (Atlanta: Scholars Press, 1986). Text 4QpaleoExod^{m} is the thirteenth Exodus scroll from Cave 4, written in paleo-Hebrew script. "Paleo-Hebrew" refers to the pre-exilic script of ancient Israel that was later displaced by the so-called square script used in most of the Dead Sea Scrolls. Paleo-Hebrew was used after the Babylonian exile but less frequently than the square script. The Samaritans used it exclusively for their Bibles, and several biblical texts from Qumran—including the fairly lengthy *Leviticus Scroll* from Cave 11—are written in paleo-Hebrew script.

2. His theory was developed over a series of articles. A summary can be found in his *Ancient Library of Qumran and Modern Biblical Studies,* 188–94. See also the essays collected in *Qumran and the History of the Biblical Text,* ed. Cross and Talmon (Cambridge: Harvard University Press, 1975). Cross' argument arose out of the observations of his teacher, W. F. Albright (see *BASOR* 140 [1955]).

3. See Bruce Metzger, R. C. Dentan, and W. Harrelson, *The Making of the New Revised Standard Version of the Bible* (Grand Rapids: Eerdmans, 1991), 25–27. The quotation given above is from the NRSV.

4. Emanuel Tov, "A Modern Textual Outlook Based on the Qumran Scrolls," *Hebrew Union College Annual* 53 (1982): 11–27.

5. Emanuel Tov, *Textual Criticism of the Hebrew Bible* (Minneapolis: Fortress, 1992), 114–17.

6. J. Sanders, "The Dead Sea Scrolls—A Quarter Century of Study," *Biblical Archaeologist* 36 (1973): 140.

7. The Hebrew canon of Scripture is as follows: *Law:* Genesis, Exodus, Leviticus, Deuteronomy. *Prophets:* Joshua, Judges, Samuel, Kings, Isaiah, Jeremiah, Ezekiel, the Twelve (minor prophets). *Writings:* Psalms, Proverbs, Job, Ruth, Song of Solomon, Ecclesiastes, Lamentations, Esther, Daniel, Ezra, Nehemiah, Chronicles.

Index of Modern Authors